MOUNTAIN BIKING in Southwest Idaho

By Stephen Stuebner
and Stephen Phipps

Produced by High Mountain Adventures

ACKNOWLEDGMENTS

The authors wish to express special thanks to our wives, Amy Stahl and Sarah Phipps, for their assistance, encouragement and tolerance. We want to thank everyone else who helped make this book possible, including Greg Harley and Jan Sutter, Glenn Oakley, Sally Stevens, Ken Snider, Alan Russell, Jim Woodward, Vickie Lawson, Cliff Wilcox, Dale Sweet, Alan Marriage, Rick Gerrard, Chris Haunold, Mike Cooley, Tom Platt, Bruce Reichert, Denise DeCoster, Lea Cooper, Dan Popkey, George Farrow, Tim Breuer and Bob Wood.

CREDITS

Cover photo: Glenn Oakley

Cover design: Sally Stevens

Computer mapping: Greg Harley

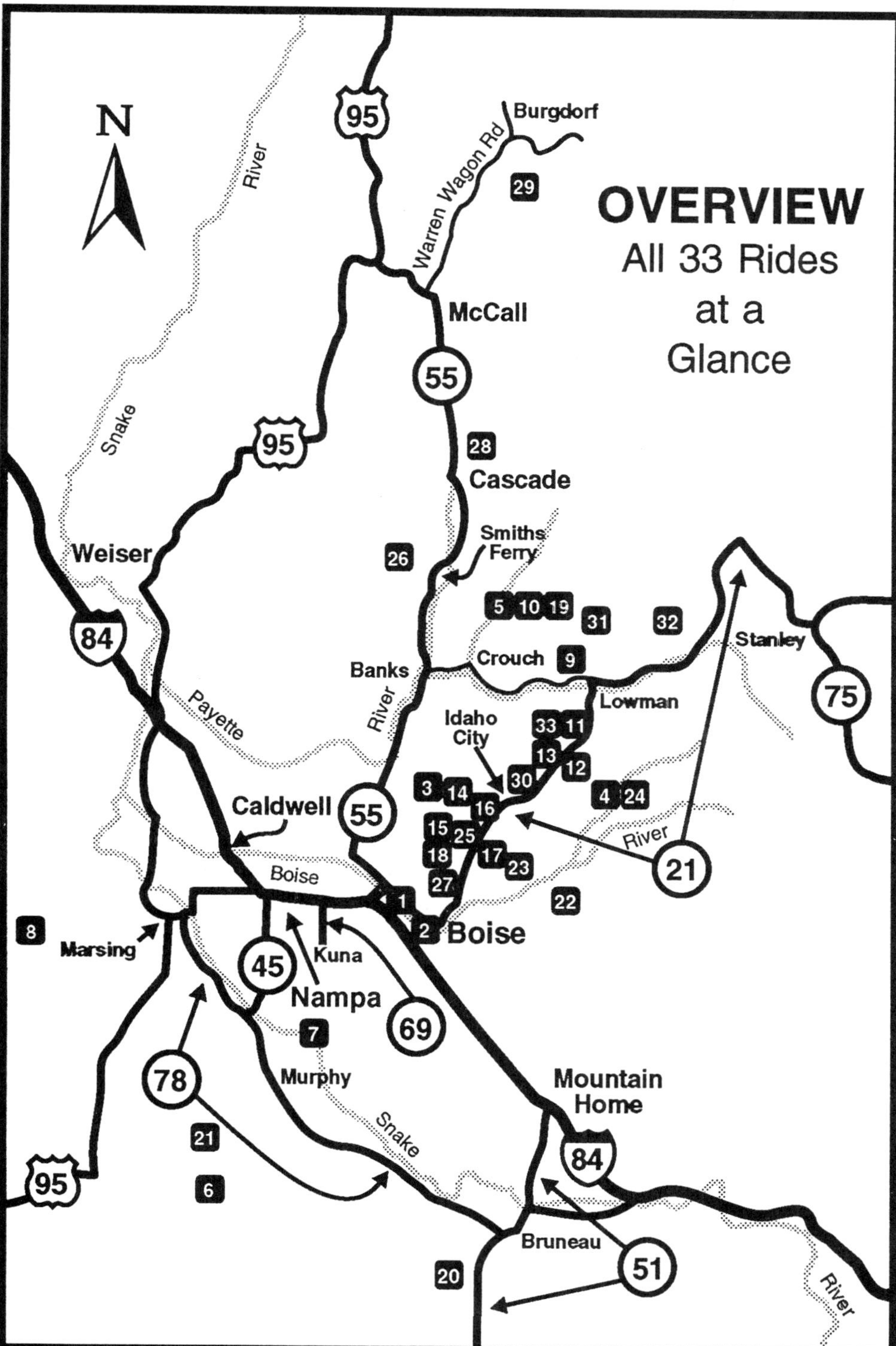

OVERVIEW
All 33 Rides
at a
Glance
N
River
Snake
Payette
River
Boise
Snake
River
Burgdorf
Warren Wagon Rd
McCall
Cascade
Smiths Ferry
Banks
Crouch
Lowman
Stanley
Idaho City
Weiser
Caldwell
Marsing
Kuna
Nampa
Boise
Murphy
Mountain Home
Bruneau
95
55
84
75
21
45
69
78
51
1
2
3
4
5
6
7
8
9
10
11
12
13
14
15
16
17
18
19
20
21
22
23
24
25
26
27
28
29
30
31
32
33

TABLE OF CONTENTS

THE RIDES

BEGINNER

INTERMEDIATE

EXPERT/ADVANCED

FORWARD

Back in the 1880s, when the mountain bike was invented, back before asphalt was even a bituminous gleam in a Scotsman's eye, all roads were rutted dirt carriage routes or narrow footpaths by turns either dusty or muddy. Barely anyone ventured more than 10 miles from their birthplace, and only the coachmen and drovers knew how to really get about, since maps were not made in mass printings. Travel was a cumbersome, tedious and expensive luxury.

Then came the safety bicycle, a user-friendly cousin of the high-wheeler. Within a decade, they were everywhere, affordable to even the blue-collar laborers and women, requiring no stable, no livery and no food. They were likened to two-wheeled instruments of the devil, and laws were quickly enacted requiring a runner waving a red flag to precede any cyclist venturing into certain towns to warn the populace and prepare the drivers and their nervous teams. The social order was in the process of being ruptured, for anyone with a sense of adventure and a bicycle that cost a month's wages could cruise the rich part of town after work or on the weekend, and venture "abroad," learning about the neighboring towns and cities without blowing a wad of dough and spending a week in transit.

This drama has been re-enacted in Marin County beginning in the mid-1970s with exuberant young riders encroaching on the formerly secret trails of the leisure class. A few of the riders could have used a flag man, but most of them were barely noticed since the green spaces in the county had not yet filled up with fitness boomers. Due to a very unfortunate coincidence of political corruption, and input from a few influential people, rules were passed (without the encumbrance of due process) barring bicycles from trails narrower than 15 feet across. This would not matter to you folks in Boise and southern Idaho, except that it could happen to you.

As hard as it may be to understand, there is a reason for anti-bike sentiment: the bikes feel foreign to other trail users. New. Weird. Scary. And cyclists in the Boise Front aren't taking enough precautions to make a good first impression.

I predict that unless mountain cyclists learn to treat other trail users with more respect, town parks, private parcels, easements and foothills canyons could be off-limits to mountain bicyclists within five years. It could end up being your favorite trails, the ones where you ride after work to de-stress. My ride on a Monday evening in October revealed all I needed to know. Large herds of cyclists buzz through the draws and routinely clear the path with a yell or the squeal of poorly adjusted brakes. Think how inconvenient it is to come up on a group of 20 hikers hogging the trail, perhaps all transfixed by a hawk sighting. Now just trade shoes.

When I refer to a large group of cyclists, I mean more than 4 people.

My RX for instant, mutual respect on the local trails of Boise is this:

■Always assume there is someone around a blind turn. You're near a big town with lots of outdoor friends like yourself. Go ahead and get up to speed only where you can see there is no one ahead. Slow down before the turns.

■Maintain traction at all times, resist the urge to skid. It leaves a calling card: "Bozo was here."

■Never take alternative routes to the main path in single-track rides. It is unfortunate to see a trail split several ways just to satisfy one's urge for novelty. We really look bad there (although, again, the actual erosion is negligible -- it's just crummy PR). Build up log walls to deter switchback cutting and high-berming.

■Announce your presence with a gentle cough, or if you have a bell, ring it from way back so it's not a shock. I like to let the walker or rider choose where they want to let you pass, instead of my dictating where they should go. Humans are not slalom poles to be skillfully negotiated. Besides, no one really knows if you mean "move left" or "I'm on your left" when all they heard was the word "left!" If you're with another person, simply conversing alerts others, provided you are going nice and slow. When someone scowls at you, realize they've had a bad experience and are projecting it on you, grant them some dignity and don't scowl back.

■Ride slowly and well-spaced (several bike lengths between riders) for the part of the ride that is within three miles of any parking lot. As a rule, weekday hikers and their dogs seldom go beyond a six-mile roundtrip.

■Refrain from group training rides except at unusual times like 7 a.m., and never on weekends. Race on weekends.

■Experimental Etiquette Zones (carved wooden signs made by local high school shop students) should be immediately posted to remind people that excruciatingly polite behavoir can be turned on like one's headlights in daylight test areas. The entire Greenbelt should be one such zone, and public awareness of this should be heightened, popularized. All those skaters, walkers, cyclists and joggers act as if they are the only people on the path, stopping to socialize (there's no law against it) or swerving wildly to avoid one another. It should be neutral, low-speed, car-free peddling and never used as a time trial training route. It is for recreation, right? Remember that the children learning to ride and the grannies getting reacquainted with two wheels ride there -- they'll graduate to dirt, but they should feel safe on the bike path, for heaven's sake.

■Go to the next planning meeting where development of popular riding areas is being discussed, meet the local auto-intensive environmentalists (everyone who uses bikes more than cars ... oops, pardon the pigeon-holing) and ask what you, a dedicated environmentalist yourself, can do to help. Nobody wants to see Hull's Gulch packed with townhouses, except the person subdividing that juicy parcel. I think that folks in Idaho are so desperate for help to slow down development that they will accept the assistance of a mountain cyclist. This is not possible in Marin because we are so hated.

■Participate at least once a year in trail maintenance work days. They're fun and you get a great sense of accomplishment putting in water bars and smoothing ruts. Kinda makes you want to buttonhole the folks who "wreck it for everybody" and give them a good talking to.

But ... isn't it better that young people take their risks in an outdoor sport, than on the street or in a bar or worst of all on the street after being at the bar? Exactly where do you expect the rebellion to show itself? Know that thoughtlessness is a phase even you went through, and don't condemn. I always suggest to reckless riders that they come to the next race, and in the mean time, practice a little farther away from civilization. I have mastered the diplomatic delivery, and it's not easy, because you want to vent your loathing about all bad guys onto the jerk in front of you, but chances are this fellow (it's rarely a woman) doesn't have a clue that what he's doing could be construed as rude. If you must pontificate, leave the person with a way to save face, like imagining he had other things on his mind when he buzzed the birdwatcher. Oops!

Statistics don't lie. Our sport is a safe one. We only occasionally "ding" ourselves, and the reason no one has died yet riding mountain bikes in the wild, to my knowledge, is that most people ride with good common sense.

Conduct your own accident post-mortem by thinking back to your worst crash, and recall that it was something that distracted you from that tuned-in trail concentration you needed to stay upright on a mountain bike. Yep, if you hadn't spent three seconds gawking at the weed in your derailleur, your front wheel wouldn't have found that rut, you wouldn't have sailed over the handlebars, etc. Or was it turning your head to talk? Or not knowing they'd put a new ditch on the trail? All are avoidable by assuming nothing, and taking in all cues through your eyes and ears and nose, hands, feet, everything.

On a mountain bike, it's easy to feel like an animal wild and free, why become endangered? Why let your habitat shrink because of a few bad habits? Evolve!

The authors of this guidebook intend to open your eyes to the many great riding opportunities all around Boise and southwest Idaho. Savor the different terrains to the west, north, east and south of town. Prevent bike gridlock on the "Freeway" and enjoy Hulls Gulch alone on your bike and invite your friends to do our rides followed by nature's perfect restorers: pizza and beer.

-- Jacquie Phelan, Marin County, Calif., November 1992.

DISCLAIMER

WARNING: MOUNTAIN BIKING INVOLVES A NUMBER OF UNAVOIDABLE RISKS THAT MAY CAUSE SERIOUS INJURY OR DEATH. THESE RISKS INCLUDE FLYING OFF YOUR BIKE AT INOPPORTUNE MOMENTS, MECHANICAL BREAKDOWNS, AND GETTING LOST. ANYONE WHO PURCHASES THIS BOOK ASSUMES ALL RISK AND RESPONSIBILITY FOR THEIR OWN SAFETY AND WELFARE.

The authors have attempted to provide an accurate description of each route in this guidebook. However, a route listed in this book may or may not be safe for anyone to ride at any given time. Routes vary in difficulty, and abilities vary according to the experience and conditioning of each cyclist. Trails may change or deteriorate due to cataclysmic environmental or climatic events, logging, mining, wildfires, road-building or other circumstances beyond the authors' control.

The trail descriptions and other information in this book are designed to help cyclists find new places to ride and equip cyclists with the necessary information about what to bring on a ride and how to prepare for it. To complement the information provided in this book, cyclists should purchase topographic maps for the area in which they plan to ride.

Some expert routes in this book are long, difficult rides that involve lengthy first-gear climbs for hours at a time. These rides could become a nightmare for beginning and intermediate cyclists. Intermediates and beginners who attempt an expert ride do so at their own risk. Please be honest with yourself and do not attempt expert rides that are beyond your ability. Or, pick off a portion of an expert ride one piece at a time. Never embark on an expert ride late in the day -- you could break down, get caught by darkness, and spend a nasty cold night out in the woods.

Be prepared for the worst. The authors recommend cyclists carry matches, a compass, a space blanket, rain gear and extra clothes. It is imperative that you supplement this book with more detailed information on first-aid, bicycle repair, physical conditioning and wilderness survival.

Before you embark on a ride, tell someone where you are going and leave them a map of the trail. If you get lost, the Ada County Mountain Search and Rescue Team recommends that you stay put, build a fire and wait for help. The phone number for search and rescue in Ada County is 377-6790. For other counties, call the sheriff's office for the county in which the person is lost.

Know your limitations and use common sense. It's better to give up on a ride than spend an uncomfortable night in the woods. Be alert, ride under control and always wear a helmet.

INTRODUCTION

Congratulations. You now hold the key to discovering more than 30 trails in southwest Idaho. We have selected a rich blend of routes featuring a wide diversity of scenery and challenge for the full spectrum of mountain cyclists, from rank beginners to gonzo high-tech animals. No matter how long you've lived in southwest Idaho, this book likely contains rides you've never heard of or ridden before. Throughout our search for the best trails in the region, we searched for the elusive, ULTIMATE RIDE. Depending on your ability level, we're confident you'll find more than one route that fits your definition of the ULTIMATE RIDE.

How to use the book: Cyclists can improve their riding skills and endurance by selecting easy routes to begin with and then working up to more challenging trails. We have provided a complete guide to the Greenbelt so cyclists can tour the Boise River through Boise and get warmed up on asphalt. Then we selected some easy, off-pavement rides for beginners and families who have never ridden on dirt before. Some of our intermediate rides will acquaint cyclists with single-track trails, which require more agility, balance and bursts of power. As cyclists feel more comfortable on beginner or intermediate trails, we encourage you to bite off a portion of an advanced or expert ride one piece at a time. Repeated efforts will boost your skill level to the point where you can become an advanced rider.

Of course, a major key to becoming a strong rider is fitness -- getting in shape. If want to get serious about mountain cycling, we suggest that you begin training and building endurance by riding uphill for several miles at a time. For example, if you build endurance to the point where you can ride to the top of Eighth Street, Rocky Canyon Road or Bogus Basin Road in the Boise Front, you should have enough strength to ride the expert rides in the guidebook. If you ride several times a week on a consistent basis, you'll find that mountain cycling is an enjoyable, low-impact aerobic workout that's also a wonderful way to explore the mountains.

The authors suggest that you read the introductory section of the guidebook before embarking on a ride, particularly if you're new to the sport. This section includes tips on hill climbing, bike maintenance, tool kits, map legend, and the International Mountain Biking Association Rules of the Trail.

The authors emphasize the importance of following the IMBA Rules of the Trail, particularly the first two regarding responsible, shared use of trails, respecting private land and reducing environmental impacts to the maximum extent possible. We embarked on this guidebook project, in part, to give mountain cyclists new routes to ride away from the Boise foothills. As many riders know, we face the potential that authorities will close routes to mountain cycling if we do not repair damaged trails and enhance our relations with other trail users. Please do your part.

BIKE MAINTENANCE, TOOL KITS AND REPAIRS

Anyone who ventures into the backcountry for a mountain bicycling adventure must carry a basic tool kit and hand pump to fix the inevitable mechanical breakdown.

But of course, in order to repair flats or other problems, you need to learn how to perform basic maintenance tasks on your bike. Moreover, you should learn to regularly maintain your bike at home. Preventive maintenance, such as regular cleanings, cable adjustments, keeping the rims trued, replacing the bearings and replacing a worn chain, will help avoid major breakdowns on the trail. None of these tasks are difficult, but if you don't know how to maintain your bike, there are several books available.[1]

We recommend carrying a fairly extensive tool kit in your vehicle when going out on a ride, and bringing along the bare essentials on the ride itself.

Recommended tool kit for your vehicle:

hand pump (preferably an upright, powerful one)
extra tube
spokes
tire irons
patch kit
chain tool
chain lube
spoke wrench
headset tool
brake cables
derailleur cables
extra chain links
crescent wrench
hex wrenches
allen wrenches
freewheel remover
crank bolts
bearings
screwdrivers

---

[1]We suggest these repair manuals:

"Mountain Bike Maintenance -- Repairing and Maintaining the Off-Road Bicycle" by Rob Van der Plas (Bicycle Books-San Francisco, 1992)

"The Mountain Bike Repair Handbook" by Dennis Coello (Lyons & Burford, 1990)

Recommended bare-essential tool kit:

hand pump
extra tube
one tire iron
chain tool
allen wrenches
patch kit
spoke wrench
chain lube (optional)
combination tools, such as "Cool Tool" or Performance Versa-T tool

Recommended safety gear

rain gear
first-aid kit
compass
lighter or matches
space blanket
topographic map

HINTS ON DEALING WITH MAJOR BREAKDOWNS

Problem: Broken rear derailleur
Solution: Create a one-speed with your chain tool

Open up a chainlink with the chain tool, shorten the chain and bypass the non-functional rear derailleur. Put your chain on the middle chain ring in the front and in the middle ring of your rear sprocket. This creates a one-speed bike that you'll be able to ride home.

Problem: Frequent flat tires due to thorns or "goat heads"
Solution: "Slime" or new tube

Desert lands in southwest Idaho often contain goat head bushes, a noxious plant that spreads ball-shaped seeds containing nail-like spikes. In an especially unlucky situation, you can fly off the trail and end up with 20 punctures in your tire tube. There are two ways to combat this problem: 1) Take your wheel to the bike shop and have them inject each tube with about 4 ounces of liquid tire sealant, known as "slime." After running over goat heads, spin your wheel and the slime will automatically seal the holes. Then pump up the tire; 2) Carry an extra tube. Note: If you run over a goat head, but it doesn't cause a flat, sometimes it's better to leave it there until you get home.

Problem: You get a flat, and your friend's pump (the only one you have with you) only works for Presta valves.

Solution: Carry a valve adapter in your tool kit so you borrow someone's pump regardless of whether it works for Presta or Schrader valves.

Problem: You get a flat, and a rider comes by and offers you an extra tube with a Schrader valve. But your rims only take Presta valves.
Solution: Have a local bike shop drill your rims so you can use either type of valves in a pinch.

CLIMBING UPHILL IN THE MOUNTAINS

Riding a mountain bike in the mountains of southwest Idaho -- even in the Boise Front -- usually involves a fair amount of uphill climbing. Yes, riding hills is difficult and challenging. It makes your heart race, it makes your thighs burn, it makes you sweat, and sometimes, it hurts.

However, there's a method to the madness. It's called Zen and the Art of Climbing Hills. To master the basic technique of hill climbing requires the correct mental attitude, learning how to gear down quickly, deft adjustments in body position, preserving your strength on long rides and the broad use of gears in general.

First, even if you find hills intimidating, you've got to develop the right mental attitude about hill climbing. Why did you buy a mountain bike? To ride in the mountains, of course. You don't want to be a spectator, you want to be a participant. You're going to have to ride into the mountains to get that new bike muddy, those new bike tights dirty and show your neighbors that you're a real animal. You dream of getting in good enough shape to climb roads and trails to a mountain peak where you can see for 100 miles in all directions. You yearn to be able to keep up with your friends, and even better, to have a pair of sleek, muscle-toned legs.

Well, just like anything else, you've got to pay your dues. There's no free lunch. But hey, we've got some good news: the mountain bicycle was built especially for climbing hills. Unlike the one-speed bike you rode as a kid, mountain bikes have a huge range of gears, usually at least 18 speeds and up to 24. That means you'll be able to climb most any hill on a two-wheel-drive dirt road in the mountains; it's just a matter of how fast you go, and how long your legs can handle the grade before you get pooped.

The most important thing to remember in riding hills is the higher you climb, the longer you'll be able to scream downhill and revel in one gigantic head rush. Ahah! That's why gonzo mountain bikers love to climb so much: they love to get a great workout, and they're always seeking a big downhill rush.

OK, now you're ready to build up a sweat, burn some calories and get in shape. Start by riding a continuous, predictable grade like Table Rock Road, Eighth Street extension or Rocky Canyon Road in the Boise Front.

Proper gear selection is essential in riding hills. You want to carry as much momentum from the flats or a downhill into the climb. Stay in a big gear until you start feeling the hill in your legs, then gear down slowly, one or two gears at a time until you reach the comfort zone. If you face an abrupt, steep climb after a steep downhill, however, you'll have to drop into an easy gear right before the steep climb begins. This takes anticipation, practice and experience to know what gears you can push on a particular grade. If in doubt, drop into your lowest gear.

There's another reason why you have to drop into an easy gear prior to a steep climb -- your chain won't shift very easily when you're cranking up an abrupt hill. The trick here is to let up on the pedals as you shift and then resume the pressure on the pedals.

Correct body position is another key part of climbing on dirt roads and trails to prevent the rear tire from spinning out. Experience will teach you that spinning out can be avoided in most instances by shifting your butt back slightly on the saddle. If it's steep enough that the front wheel starts popping up off the ground, slide forward a little. On steep spots with good traction, you may need to stand on the pedals and lean over the handlebars to keep the front wheel on the ground. However, it's best to stay seated as much as possible because many trails will be too loose to allow standing on the peddles. You'll spin out and waste energy.

When you purchase a mountain bike, pay attention to the chain ring sizes in the front sprockets and back cluster. Average riders should start with front chain ring sizes of 24, 34 and 46 teeth. The rear cluster should range from 13 to 30 teeth.

More climbing tips:

■Relax, rarely will you need a death grip on the handle bars.

■Install toe clips or step-in pedals for efficient riding.

■Practice proper breathing technique. When you find yourself breathing hard, take very deep breaths and then, purse your lips and exhale slowly. This technique helps pump more oxygen into your body and gives you more climbing and staying power.

■Make sure your seat is adjusted properly for maximum power (your knees should be slightly bent at full extension).

■Spin easy gears to avoid burning up all your energy in the first hill; as you get in better shape, try to push bigger gears. But be careful! Pushing big gears on steep hills may lead to a myriad of injuries.

■Concentrate when riding on single-track trails; a small obstacle such as a bush, tree root or rock may force you off your bike. In order to avoid this, look ahead for obstacles.

■Buy climbing bar-ends for your handlebars to keep your weight over your front wheel in steep sections.

■Reduce tire pressure for better traction on loose dirt; however, be sure to follow the tire pressure guidelines for minimum and maximum inflation (it's etched on the side of the tire).

■Install index shifting levers on your bike; it's easier to shift into low gears in steep sections in a pinch.

■Always drink plenty of water -- it enhances endurance, and prevents dehydration and cramps.

DOWNHILL RIDING TIPS

Downhill riding requires proper technique, the right mental attitude, and well-adjusted brakes. Skill and attitude are the factors that determine confidence or the lack of it.

Before flying down a mountain out of control, take the time to master some basic skills in riding downhill. Begin by learning to respect the power of your front brake. It's OK to use the front brake during descents, but use it with caution. On steep drops, a tight grip on the front brake will pitch the cyclist over the handlebars.

When learning to ride downhill, lower your seat-post several inches. With the seat out of the way, it will be easier to shift your center of gravity toward the back tire. It helps prevent flipping over the handlebars, too. Also, shift into a higher gear -- this prevents the chain from slapping against your bike and prevents it from falling off. The ideal gear setting is the big ring in front and a middle gear in back.

In general, when riding downhill, keep your speed in check by using the front and back brakes, and keep your weight toward the rear of the bike, sometimes behind your seat and over the back tire. It's best to use only both brakes when riding straight trail sections, not on curves. Apply most of your weight over the pedals, which should be positioned in parallel fashion at 3 and 9 o'clock. Keep your legs and arms bent, and relax -- let them absorb shock.

A word about front shocks: adding a shock absorber to your front fork will reduce the impact on your arms and wrists and allow you to ride faster downhill. However, shocks are no substitute for good technique.

More downhill tips:

■Always wear a helmet.

■Wear gloves to help cushion a fall, and wear sunglasses to keep the bugs out of your eyes.

■Try moderate hills first before you try big steeps. The key is to start small and work up to more technical descents.

■On steep drops, use only the back brake and feather it to avoid skidding and causing erosion. Feathering is accomplished by rapidly squeezing and releasing the brake repeatedly.

■When encountering obstacles such as deep sand, rocks, logs and creeks, use only the rear brake to slow down. Using the front brake will cause the front wheel to lock up and eject the rider over the handlebars into the "Superman" flying position.

■Stand on the pedals through rough terrain, keeping your weight toward the rear of the bike. Carry some speed through rocky or sandy areas; it helps keep your balance.

■If the descent looks too steep, stop and get off the bike. It may be too dangerous to ride.

■The harder you apply your brakes, the farther you should shift your weight to the rear of the bike.

■Learn to bunny-hop or wheelie over rocks and other obstacles. The key is to lift with your pedals and arms prior to the obstacle and pre-jump.

IMBA RULES OF THE TRAIL

1. Ride on open trails only. Respect trail and road closures (ask if you're not sure), avoid possible trespass on private land, obtain permits and authorization as may be required. Federal and state wilderness areas are closed to mountain bikes.

2. Leave no trace. Be sensitive to the dirt beneath you. Even on open trails, you should not ride under conditions where you will leave evidence of your passing, such as on certain soils shortly after a rain. Observe the different types of soils and trail construction; practice low-impact cycling. This also means staying on the trail and not creating any new ones. Be sure to pack out at least as much as you pack in.

3. Control your bicycle! Inattention for even a second can cause disaster. Excessive speed maims and threatens people; there is no excuse for it!

4. Always yield the trail. Make known your approach well in advance. A friendly greeting (or a bell) is considerate and works well; startling someone may cause loss of trail access. Show your respect when passing others by slowing to a walk or even stopping. Anticipate that other trail users may be around corners or in blind spots.

5. Never spook animals. All animals are startled by an unannounced approach, a sudden movement, or a loud noise. This can be dangerous for you, for others, and for the animals. Give animals extra room and time to adjust to you. In passing, use special care and follow the directions of horseback riders (ask if uncertain). Running cattle or disturbing wild animals is a serious offense. Leave gates as you found them, or as marked.

6. Plan ahead. Know your equipment, your ability, and the area in which you are riding -- and prepare accordingly. Be self-sufficient at all times. Wear a helmet, keep your machine in good condition, and carry necessary supplies for changes in weather or other conditions. A well-executed trip is a satisfaction to you and not a burden or offense to others.

(Reprinted courtesy of the International Mountain Bicycling Association, Route 2, Box 303, Bishop, Calif., 93514)

A WORD ABOUT CYCLOCOMPUTERS

Mileages for this guidebook have been logged with cyclocomputers. For maximum guidance, we recommend that cyclists follow the routes with a cyclocomputer or odometer. Without one, you will have extreme difficulty finding the correct route on longer rides with multiple junctions.

Cyclocomputers are not essential for the beginner rides in the book.

However, please recognize that cyclocomputers must be calibrated to the size of your wheel and tire pressure. Even after doing that, the computers will not be accurate to the exact tenth of a mile. Experienced riders with cyclocomputers know that their mileage will not always match their cycling partner's mileage. Therefore, you should not expect that your mileage will always match up exactly with that of our guidebook.

To match up as close as possible, be sure to calibrate your computer carefully.

POISON IVY

Poison Ivy is an ubiquitous plant in southwest Idaho -- it's frequently seen growing along creek bottoms, draws and trails. The ovate-shaped leaves of the three-leafed plant excrete oily resins. If poison ivy comes into contact with your skin, it can cause major rashes that itch, bubble and excrete oily puss. A poison ivy rash may take weeks to go away.

The best way to avoid getting poison ivy is to learn how to identify the plant and stay away from it.

If you accidentally touch poison ivy, or fall into a patch of it, there are a few things you can do to avoid or minimize a skin rash. Experts recommend washing the exposed areas with cold water and soap. It is important to wash all the clothes exposed as well as your bike. But people who are very susceptible to a poison ivy skin rash may not be able to wash it off.

If you see a rash break out, consult your physician. Severe rashes can be treated with various drugs. Over-the-counter, anti-itch medications are available as well.

As a preventative self-defense measure, people can apply a barrier lotion before leaving on a ride. "Armor" lotion or "Stoko-gard" are recommended.

KEY TO RIDE DESCRIPTIONS

About our rating system: For each ride, the authors have used a number of parameters to give mountain bikers a wealth of information at a glance. We hope the indications of quality, distance, difficulty and riding time will help cyclists determine whether they can accomplish a ride, and enjoy it. Below, we define the terms listed at the top of each ride:

Quality: How the ride compares to other rides in the guidebook in an overall sense. Included in this determination are the quality of mountain setting, how much shade or vegetation is present, the variety of riding conditions, surfaces and amount of climbing involved, the type of climbing involved (if you have to hike, the ride loses a few points), the quality of panoramic views, and the amount of vehicle traffic encountered along the way. We realize that quality is a subjective term, and and that cyclists will form their own opinions.

Distance: Total distance from start to finish. Some rides indicate the mileage one-way if it is an up-and-back type ride.

Difficulty: Rides are organized in this book according to ability. We broke down ability to three basic categories: beginner, intermediate and advanced/expert. We defined a beginner for the purposes of this book as someone who recently purchased a mountain bike, and has a little off-pavement experience. A beginner is expected to have very little training and endurance. Intermediate riders have been defined as those who ride off-pavement frequently, but they are still working on building skills and endurance. Advanced and expert riders should have several years of experience on a mountain bike, well-honed climbing and downhill skills and have the capacity to ride at strenuous levels for several hours at a time. We encourage riders to try more difficult rides as they develop new skills and endurance.

Riding time: The amount of time required to complete the ride for the ability prescribed. The times are listed as a range to indicate that weaker riders may take longer than others.

Trail: Riding surface -- 2-wheel-drive dirt road, 4-wheel-drive dirt road, single-track trail or hike-a-bike. All riding surfaces are dirt unless indicated otherwise.

Season: The time of year when the ride can be completed. In many cases, the season will depend on when the snow melts from the high country. Be sure to check on snow conditions before embarking on a high-altitude ride in May.

Cautions: Some rides indicate special issues of concern, such as tall brush, heavy vehicle traffic, rattlesnakes, etc.

Topo map: The name of the U.S. Geological Survey quad map if riders are interested in carrying a detailed elevation map. Along with a compass, topo maps are handy for orienteering and charting your exact location if you get lost.

Map Legend

Paved Road
Dirt Road
Single Lane Track
Alternate Route
Greenbelt Path
Greenbelt Alternate Route

84 Interstate Highway

95 US Highway

21 State Highway

377 Forest Service Road

Direction of Travel Indicator

6,000' Elevation Marker

S F S-F Trail Start/Finish Indicators

BEGINNER RIDES

THE BOISE RIVER GREENBELT

Quality: ***
Distance: 16.6 miles
Difficulty: Easy -- all abilities
Riding time: 1-2 hours one-way
Trail: Paved path, dirt path
Season: Year-round, weather permitting
Cautions: Yield to other users: walkers, joggers, roller-bladers, skiers.
Topo map: Boise South

The Boise River Greenbelt is one of the finest urban trails in the Northwest. Thanks to the tireless efforts of far-seeing, dedicated Boise residents and businesses, an extensive public pathway system has been reserved along the Boise River through most of Boise and portions of Garden City. At the time of our publication, the path extended 16.6 miles from Glenwood Street in the west side of Boise to Discovery State Park and Lucky Peak Dam, about eight miles east of town. The path weaves along the river through eight major parks and Warm Springs Golf Course. Future plans call for expanding the pathway system from Glenwood to Eagle Island State Park. Who knows, maybe it will reach Parma someday? We urge Greenbelt users to help civic leaders realize that goal.

Starting from Glenwood and heading east, we will guide you on a Greenbelt journey through Boise to Discovery Park, while noting points of interest along the way. We organized our guide to the Greenbelt in segments, showing cyclists the best places to jump on the path throughout the route. By following our guide, which includes crossing the river at several key points, cyclists can take advantage of underpasses beneath busy streets and enjoy a leisurely ride away from highways and traffic for the entire route.

Along the Greenbelt, watch for the wide variety of wildlife that resides in the cottonwood-lined river environment at different times of the year, such as songbirds, ducks and geese, great blue herons, bald eagles, beavers and deer.

GREENBELT ETIQUETTE: The Greenbelt is used by a wide variety of folks -- walkers, race-walkers, joggers, bird-watchers, anglers, the Happy Hoofers (a large clan of friendly, brisk-walking seniors), cyclists of all stripes, and roller bladers. At times, particularly on summer weekends, the Greenbelt gets crowded, causing traffic jams and potential conflicts with other users. We urge mountain bikers to treat other trail users with a heap of courtesy and respect. That means slowing down when approaching walkers and joggers -- **pedestrians have the right of way**. Let walkers and joggers know when you're approaching so you don't spook them. Sometimes you have to shout because many walkers and joggers are listening to music while they exercise. Please ride at a slow speed, particularly in the city limits. If you're racing to get somewhere, take the highway.

GLENWOOD STREET TO WILLOW LANE PARK

Distance: 1.5 miles

Start: Drive or ride your bike to the intersection of the Boise River and Glenwood Street. The path begins on the south bank of the river adjacent to the Western Idaho Fairgrounds, Boise Hawks playing field and Les Bois Park. There is ample parking at the path entrance.

Follow the path in an easterly direction. Riders will see hundreds of horse stables behind Les Bois Park. At 8/10ths of a mile, riders come to a steel bridge crossing a channel of the Boise River; turn left and follow the path across the bridge. (In the future, Garden City hopes to complete the paved path on the river's south side to the Red Lion-Riverside. But today, it dead ends soon after the bridge).

The Greenbelt crosses a second bridge at the 1 mile point and joins a paved path on the north side of the river adjacent to a Plantation subdivision. At the bridge, an interpretive sign tells the history of **Pierce Park**, an 185-acre amusement park and artificial lake developed by W.E. Pierce in 1907.

Proceed on the paved path in an easterly direction. In a quarter-mile, riders will leave the asphalt and enter an undeveloped section of the Greenbelt behind Lake Harbor. **You are now entering private property.** The authors have obtained permission from Lake Harbor for mountain cyclists to pass through the area; please stay on the gravel berm next to the river, tread lightly and respect private property. If vandalism occurs, the property may be closed to public use.

Just after the paved path ends, follow the dirt trail across a small ditch and watch for a right-hand turn into the woods along the river. It's just a few feet from the ditch. Follow the path and enjoy a short ride through the old-growth cottonwood forest. In a quarter-mile, the trail pops out on the gravel river bank for 100 feet or so to the end of Lake Harbor property and the beginning of private residences. A fenced junk heap appears on the left. **Do not turn right and cross the bridge into the woods. This is a designated walking path, and it is NOT open to bicycles. The path is reserved for foot traffic only to protect wildlife habitat and bald eagles, and to give people a rest from speeding bicycles.**

From the Lake Harbor property line, head north away from the river along the fence to Wylie Lane, where there is a gate across a dead end. Hop the gate and proceed down Wylie to James Street, turn right for two blocks and then turn left on Alamosa. Proceed to a vacant lot on the right-hand side in the middle of the block, and follow it past a brick wellhouse to Willow Lane. You have arrived at the temporary end of the existing Greenbelt.

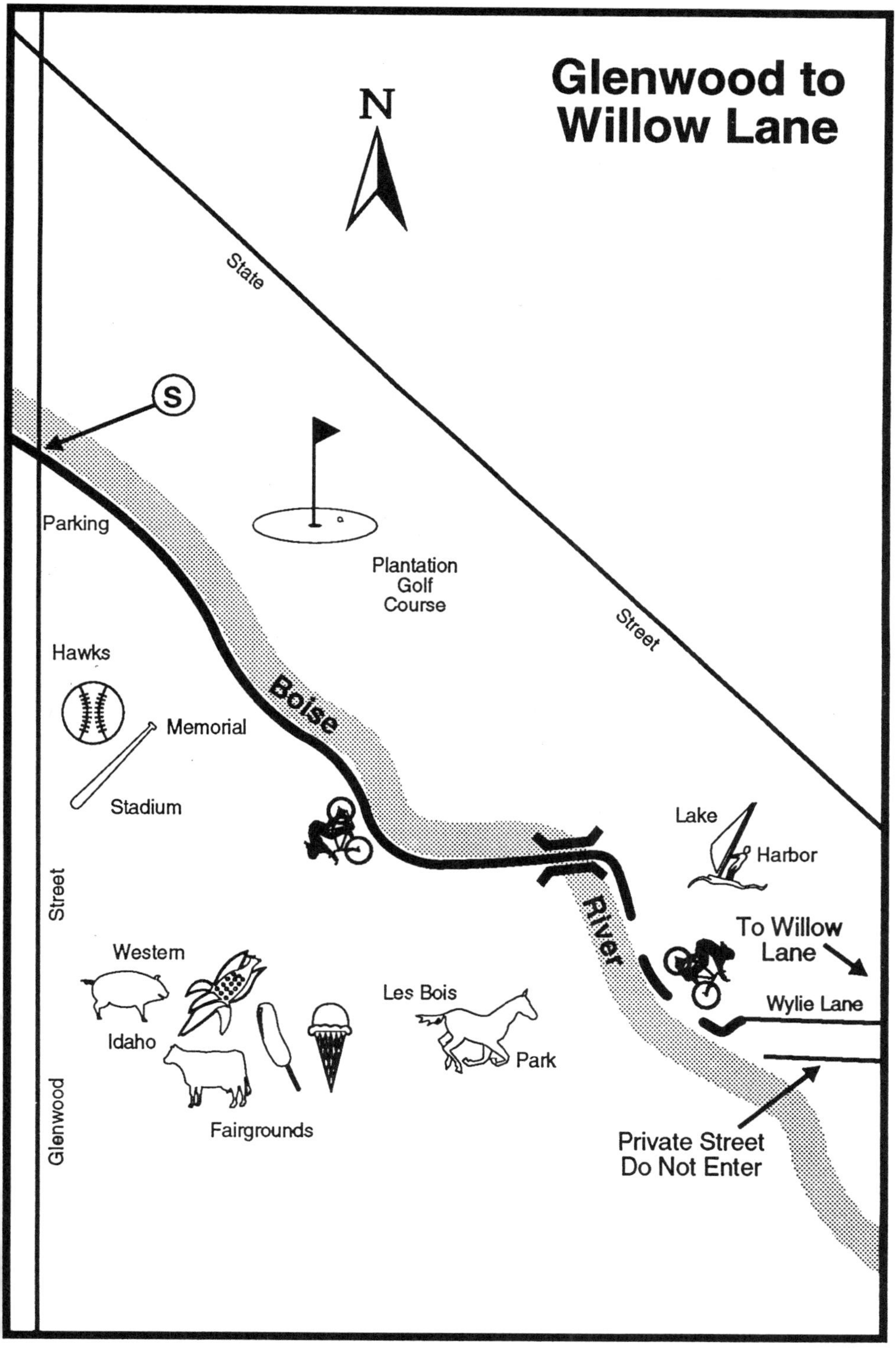
Glenwood to Willow Lane
N
State Street
S
Parking
Plantation Golf Course
Hawks Memorial Stadium
Boise River
Lake Harbor
To Willow Lane
Wylie Lane
Western Idaho Fairgrounds
Les Bois Park
Private Street Do Not Enter
Glenwood Street

WILLOW LANE TO ANN MORRISON PARK

Distance: 1.8 miles
Miles from start: 2.1

Start: Park in the large asphalt lot by the Willow Lane Athletic Fields and pick up the Greenbelt in the west end between the softball and soccer fields. Follow the path in an easterly direction. Cyclists leave the ballfields and pass by the city Water Treatment Plant on the way to Veterans State Park. The path crosses a wooden bridge and passes underneath Veterans Memorial Parkway. Now you're in Veterans Park, about 1/2 mile from Willow Lane.

Near the entrance of the park, cyclists pass an interpretive sign for **Chinese Gardens**. In the 1890s, about 1,000 Chinese watched over vast vegetable gardens at the 800-acre Davis Ranch (across the river) in what is now Garden City. Proceed on the path for 1/10th of a mile to a wooden bridge peeling off to the left toward Veterans Park. This is a good entrance or exit point for the Greenbelt. Vets Park has ample parking.

Bypass the bridge if you wish to ride on the south side of the Vets Park pond. Cross the bridge to exit the Greenbelt or if you wish to ride on the north side of the pond.

For a short family ride, people can park at Veterans Park, unload the bikes and ride toward the river and make a 1-mile loop around the pond.

The Greenbelt leaves Veterans Park across a wooden bridge heading east. Restrooms are available next to the bridge. It's 1.3 miles to Ann Morrison Park. The path follows the river's north bank and passes under Main Street, Fairview Avenue and an old railroad trestle. (Cyclists from the Bench and Garden Street area can link up with the Greenbelt via the trestle.) The path winds through Riverside Park on the north bank to the Americana underpass. Now you're riding across the river from Ann Morrison Park.

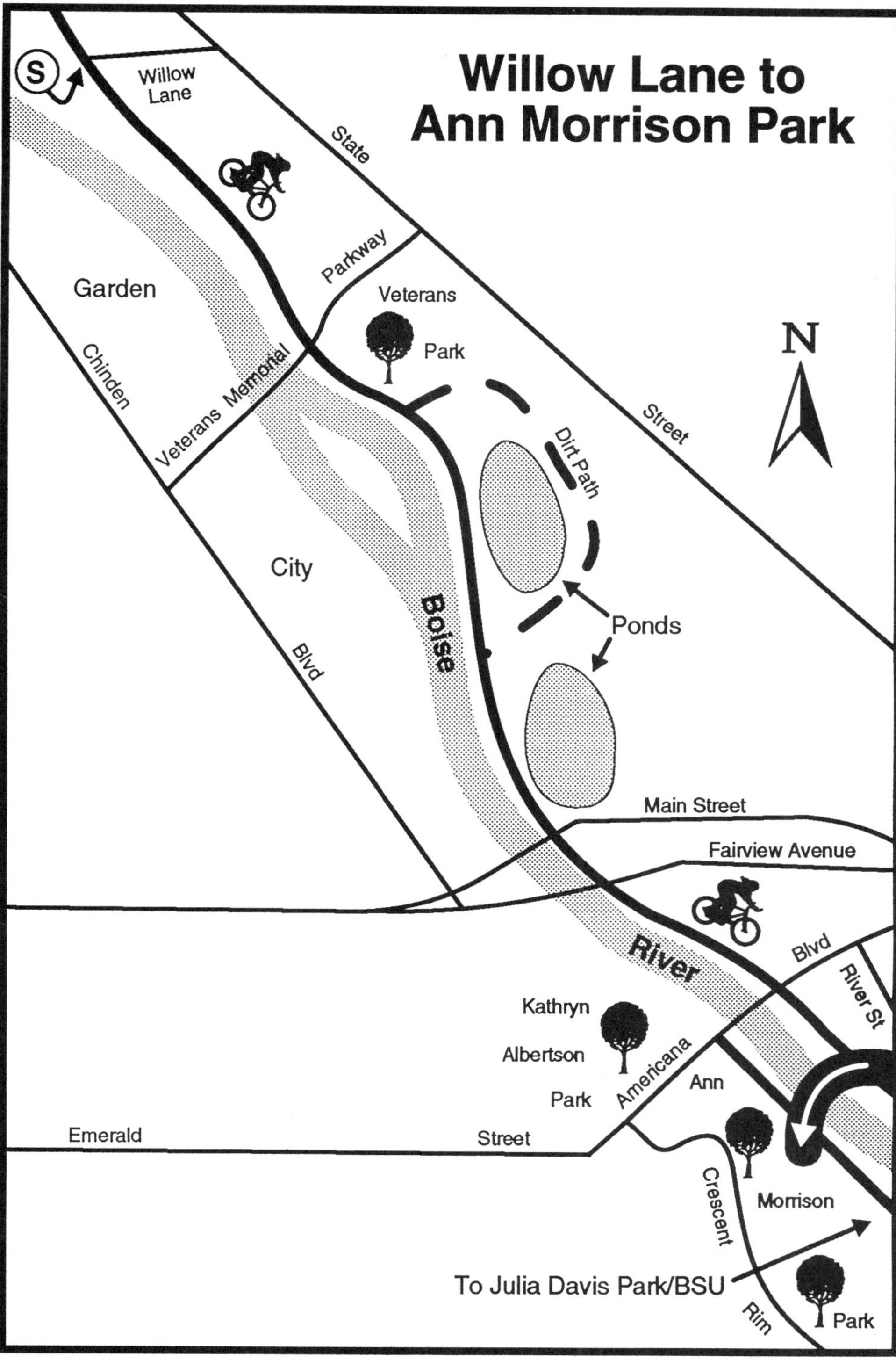
Willow Lane to Ann Morrison Park
S
Willow Lane
State
Parkway
Garden
Veterans
Park
Chinden
Veterans Memorial
N
Street
Dirt Path
City
Boise
Ponds
Blvd
Main Street
Fairview Avenue
River
Blvd
River St
Kathryn
Albertson
Park
Americana
Ann
Emerald
Street
Crescent
Morrison
To Julia Davis Park/BSU
Rim
Park

ANN MORRISON PARK TO BSU/JULIA DAVIS PARK

Distance: 1.3 miles
Miles from start: 5

Start: Parking is available on either side of the river: either in Ann Morrison Park on the south side, or by Shoreline Park and Wheels R Fun at 13th and River streets). From the Americana underpass, proceed by the rental shack to the Ann Morrison footbridge, turn right across the bridge, and turn left to proceed toward Boise State University and Julia Davis Park. **To avoid crossing Capitol Boulevard, a very busy street, it's imperative that cyclists cross the footbridge at Ann Morrison Park and ride on the south side of the river.**

For those interested in a short ride, paved bike paths wind throughout Ann Morrison Park, a vast 153-acre park with many athletic fields, a fountain and duck ponds, tennis courts and picnic areas. Ann Morrison is also the final takeout for people floating the Boise River.

Proceed through the park, and follow the tunnels underneath 9th Street and Capitol. Now you're entering the BSU campus, about 1 mile from the west end of Ann Morrison Park. Note the Morrison Center on your right. Julie Davis Park and a parallel paved path are on the other side of the river. Ride 3/10ths of a mile to the BSU Footbridge. Where you go from here depends on your interest.

To ride to ParkCenter and Spring Meadows, go straight. To reach Julia Davis Park, Municipal Park and Lucky Peak, go left and cross the bridge.

Cyclists can ride a 2-mile loop with one street crossing by starting in Ann Morrison, riding on the south bank to BSU, crossing the BSU footbridge, and riding the north bank back to Ann Morrison. From Julia Davis Park, you'll have to cross Capitol traffic and ride by the log cabin driveway to pick up the Greenbelt on the north bank.

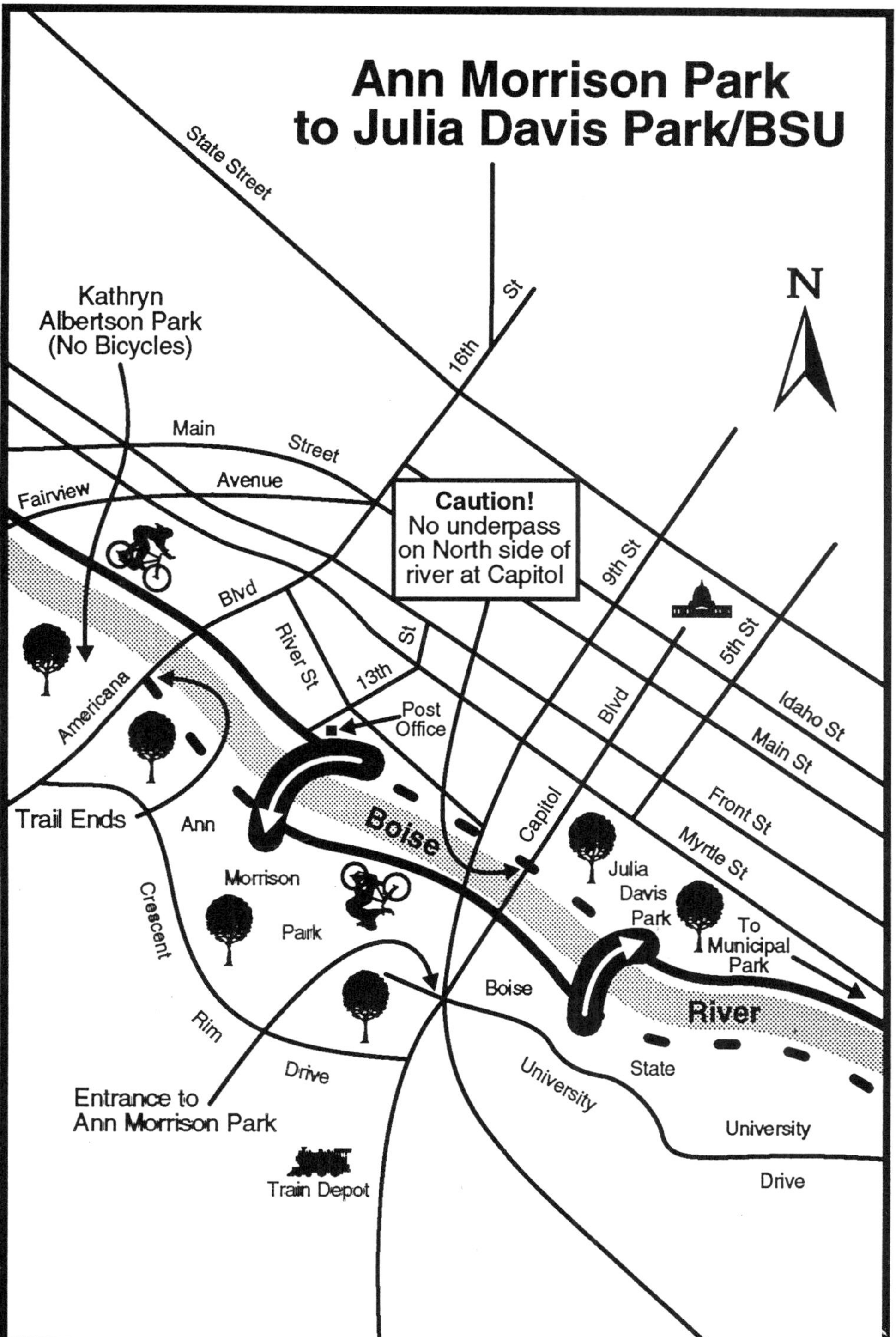
Ann Morrison Park
to Julia Davis Park/BSU
N
State Street
16th St
Kathryn
Albertson Park
(No Bicycles)
Main Street
Fairview Avenue
Blvd
Caution!
No underpass
on North side of
river at Capitol
9th St
5th St
Idaho St
Main St
Front St
Myrtle St
River St
13th St
Post
Office
Americana
Trail Ends
Ann
Morrison
Park
Crescent
Rim
Drive
Boise
River
Capitol
Blvd
Julia
Davis
Park
To
Municipal
Park
Boise
State
University
University
Drive
Entrance to
Ann Morrison Park
Train Depot

BSU TO SPRING MEADOW (Dead end)

Distance: 4 miles
Miles from start: 6

Start: Park at BSU or Julia Davis Park. Pick up the Greenbelt on the south bank of the river behind BSU and ride in an easterly direction toward ParkCenter. A half-mile from the footbridge, cyclists will pass under Broadway Street on a wide concrete path. In a few hundred yards, cross Loggers Creek on a wooden bridge to the left by an apartment complex and proceed on the south bank. Watch for the Shakespeare Festival stage on your right and a number of corporate headquarters, such as Ore-Ida and Albertson's in the ParkCenter Office Park. Here, vast lawns unfold adjacent to the Greenbelt.

Onward to the east, the path proceeds on the south bank toward Cottonwood condominiums and a small pond. Behind the condos, you will approach the entrance to the Greenbelt Wildlife Preserve and a walking path along the river. **The walking path is NOT open to bicycles. Please do not violate this closure. The path is reserved for foot traffic only to protect wildlife habitat and bald eagles, and to give people a rest from speeding bicycles.** At this junction, you've gone 2.25 miles from the BSU footbridge. Some riders may want to turn around. From here, the paved path leaves the river and winds through the subdivisions on bike lanes or lawn-bordered paths to Spring Meadow.

To proceed east, follow the paved path to a circle junction with River Run Road. Bear left and pick up the bike lane on the right-hand shoulder of the road. Stay on the bike lane about a mile to ParkCenter Boulevard. Just before the junction, turn left onto a bike path that parallels the boulevard on the left-hand side of the road. The path ends in a mile. In the future, the paved path will connect with a similar path being constructed through Wood Duck subdivision, and eventually to Eckert Road.

From here, cyclists can turn around (you've ridden 4 miles from the BSU Footbridge), or head for Eckert Road on Boise Avenue (it's a few blocks to the south), and make a loop by joining the Greenbelt path on the north side of the river. Take Boise Avenue to Eckert Road, turn left, and it's about a half-mile to the Greenbelt junction near Idaho 21.

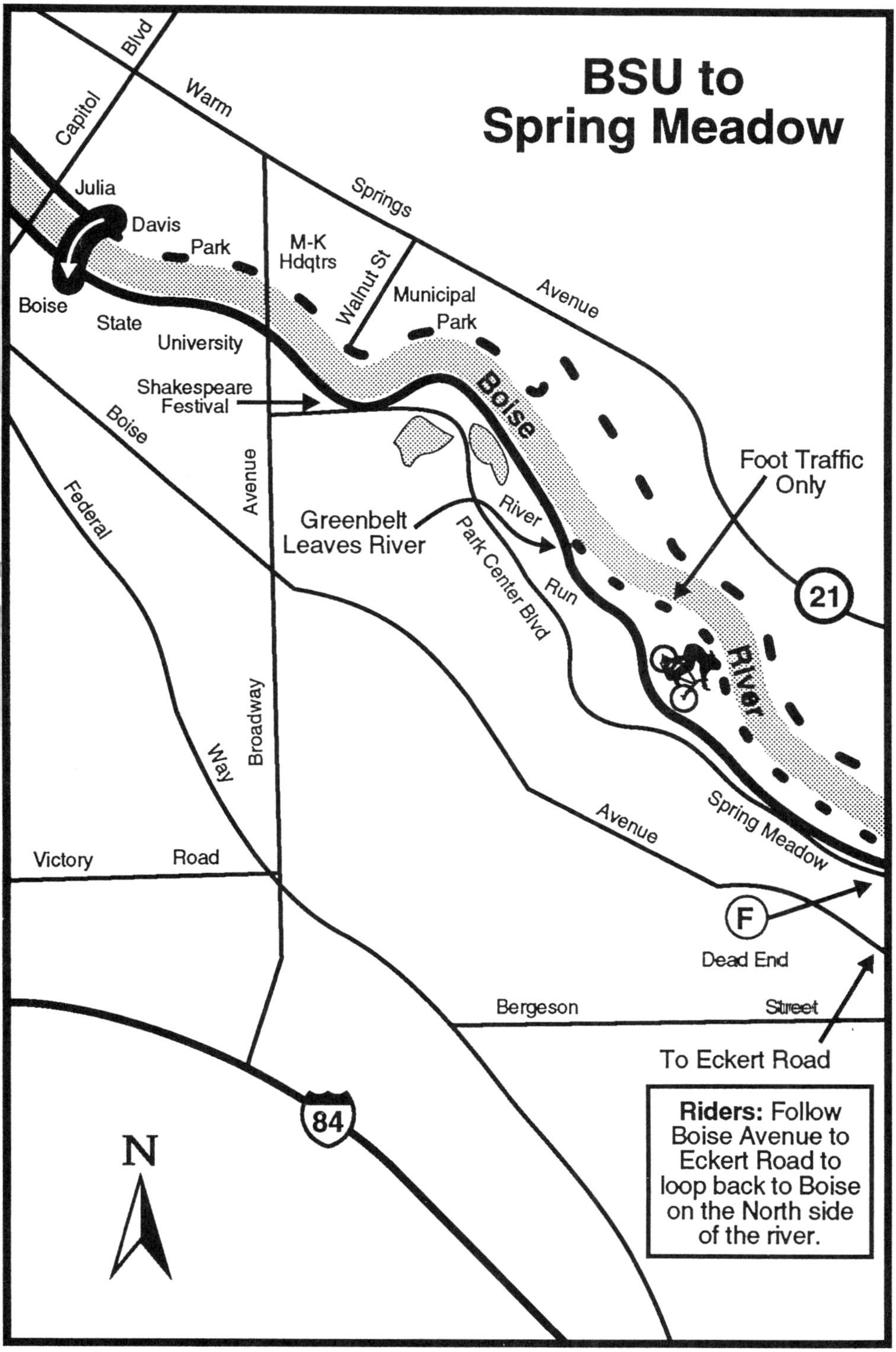
BSU to
Spring Meadow
Capitol
Blvd
Warm
Springs
Avenue
Julia
Davis
Park
M-K
Hdqtrs
Walnut St
Municipal
Park
Boise
State
University
Shakespeare
Festival
Boise
River
Boise
Avenue
Federal
Way
Broadway
Avenue
Greenbelt
Leaves River
River
Run
Park Center Blvd
Foot Traffic
Only
21
Spring Meadow
Victory
Road
F
Dead End
Bergeson
Street
To Eckert Road
84
N
Riders: Follow Boise Avenue to Eckert Road to loop back to Boise on the North side of the river.

JULIA DAVIS PARK TO MUNICIPAL PARK

Distance: 1.7 miles
Miles from start: 6

Start: Park anywhere in Julia Davis Park, one of Boise's finest. The park features a nifty playground for kids, a rose garden, band shell, zoo, tennis courts, amusement park, miniature golf, and lots of green space. Canoes and paddleboats are available for rent. Nearby adjacent to Capitol Boulevard are the Boise Art Museum and Idaho Historical Museum.

Proceed in an easterly direction toward Municipal Park. It's a half-mile from the BSU Footbridge to the Broadway Street underpass. The path follows the north bank behind Ch2M Hill to the Walnut Street exit/entrance point. Walnut Street is good place to park to jump on the Greenbelt. Onward to the east, cyclists ride by a row of attractive condos and into Municipal Park. **Riders should stop at the M-K Nature Center and check out the trophy trout in the underwater viewing areas. This is a unique opportunity.**

Past the Nature Center, an interpretive sign gives a quick history of minor league baseball in Boise. Various teams have played in the city since gold was first discovered in the Boise Basin in the 1860s.

Proceed on the paved path to a junction at the end of Municipal Park. Turn right to ride farther east to Warm Springs Golf Course, Eckert Road and Lucky Peak. Turn left to exit the Greenbelt on Walnut Street, or turn around. You've just gone 1.7 miles from the BSU Footbridge in Julia Davis Park.

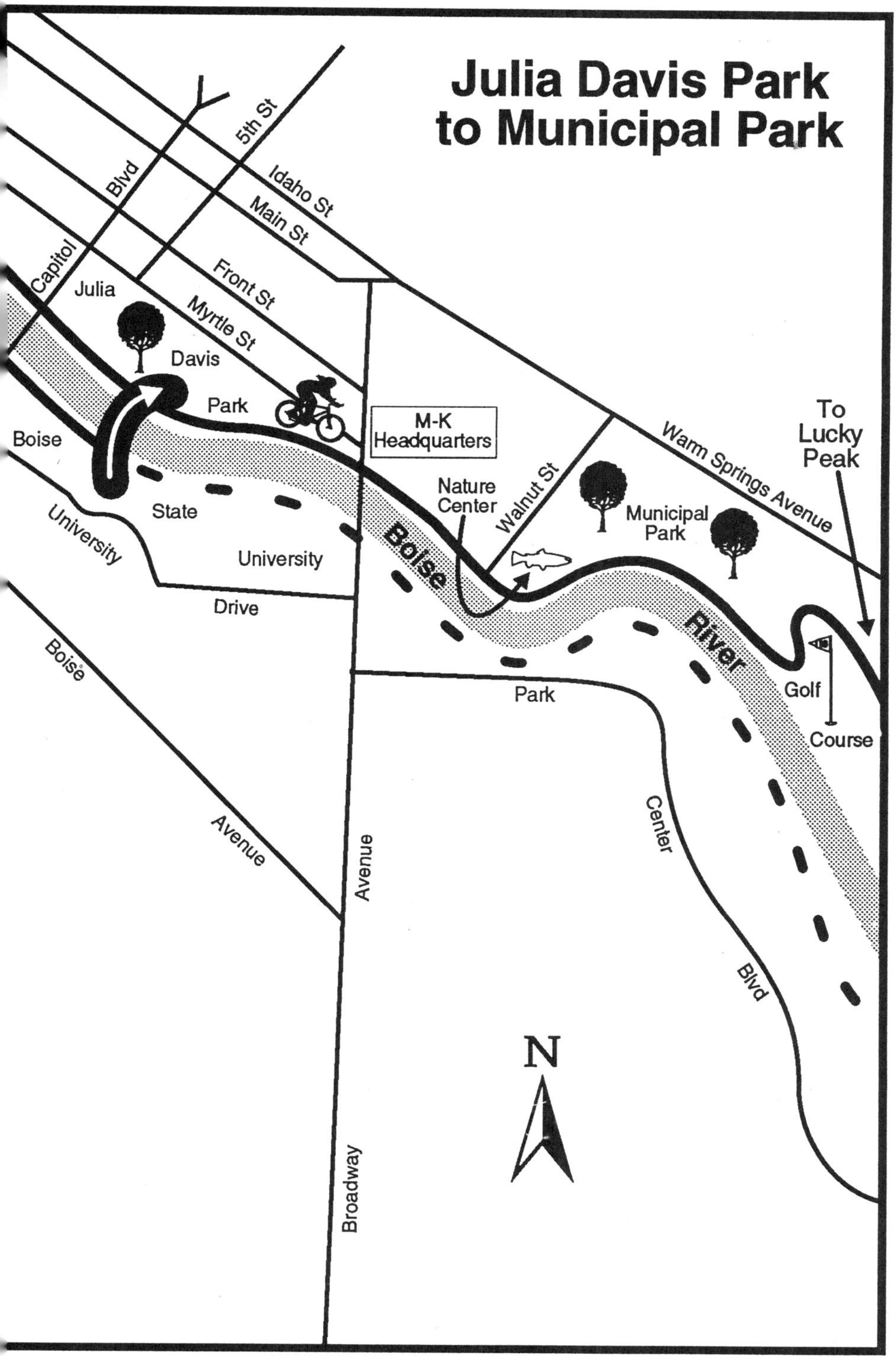
Julia Davis Park
to Municipal Park
5th St
Idaho St
Main St
Front St
Myrtle St
Capitol
Blvd
Julia
Davis
Park
Boise
State
University
University
Drive
Boise
Avenue
M-K
Headquarters
Nature
Center
Walnut St
Wam Springs Avenue
Municipal
Park
To
Lucky
Peak
Boise
River
Golf
Course
Park
Center
Blvd
Broadway
Avenue
N

MUNICIPAL PARK TO DISCOVERY STATE PARK/LUCKY PEAK DAM

Distance: 8.6 miles
Miles from start: 7.7

Start: Park in Municipal Park ("Muni"), either near Walnut Street, or in the parking lot in the center of the park. Jump on the Greenbelt and head east toward Warm Springs Golf Course. It's less than a half-mile away.

Along the way, note the interpretive sign for the **Natatorium**, a grand castle and architectural masterpiece that housed a warm springs pool, among other things, for public enjoyment. The Nat opened for business in May 15, 1892; it served the community for over 40 years. In late July 1934, a violent wind storm damaged the Nat's roof, sending a chandelier and pieces of the roof flying into the pool; luckily, no one was injured. But the Nat was condemned by city officials on Aug. 2, 1934 and demolished. A public pool remains in the same location today.

From here, the path skirts the northern edge of the golf course. Even though the city erected netting to protect cyclists, it's still possible to see errant golf balls flying by. **Be alert!**

It's 1.6 miles from Muni to the eastern edge of Warm Springs Golf Course. From here, it's clear sailing to Lucky Peak. Watch out for and yield to walkers, joggers and roller bladers.

Four miles from Muni, cyclists will cross Eckert Road. Go straight to Lucky Peak, or turn right to make a loop back to town. To complete the loop, follow Eckert Road to Boise Avenue, turn right. Follow Boise Avenue to Law Street. Turn right and follow Law to the bike path along ParkCenter Boulevard. Follow the path to the Cottonwood condos and rejoin the Greenbelt there.

For a late-evening ride to Lucky Peak, people can drive Idaho 21 to Eckert Road and park next to the Greenbelt.

Heading out to Lucky Peak from Eckert Road, cyclists ride parallel to Idaho 21 for over a mile, until the path peels off to the right on an old railroad berm looking out over Peace Valley and the Boise River. Now you're away from the highway in a high-quality segment of the path. Less than two miles from Eckert Road, you'll see a small wooden bridge cross the canal to Old Crow's Inn. It's a good place to stop for a drink, snack or meal. Some people ride the Greenbelt from town to the Old Crow's Inn for dinner. The only problem is riding home with a full stomach.

About 3 miles from Eckert Road (7 from Muni), cyclists will ride up a short hill to an overlook of Diversion Dam. This is where a big portion of the Boise River is diverted into the New York Canal to bring the Treasure Valley farms into bloom. Parking is available across Idaho 21 from the dam.

From here, it's 1.6 miles to Discovery State Park and the end of the Greenbelt. Return as you came.

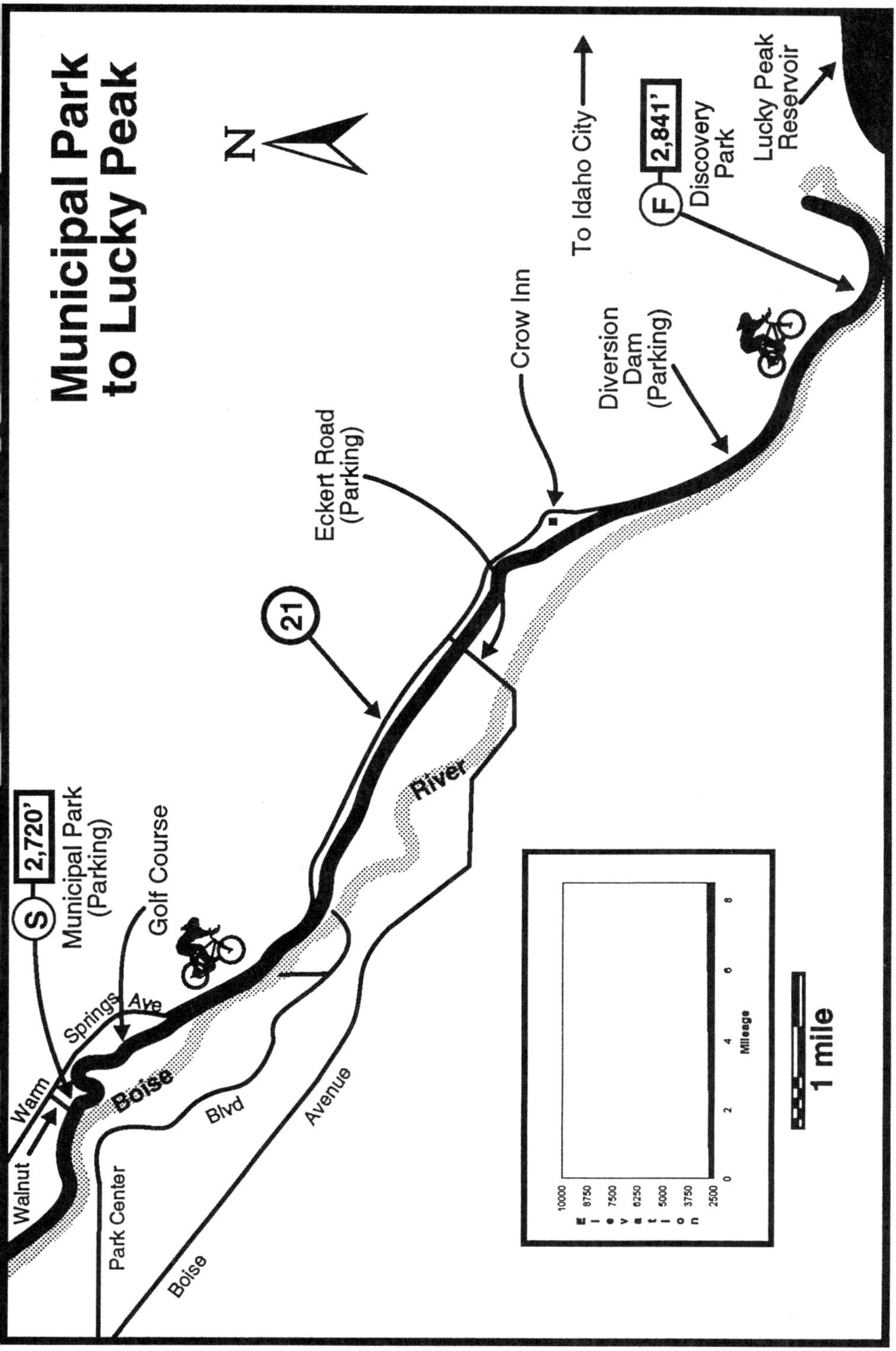

Municipal Park to Lucky Peak
N
To Idaho City
2,841'
F
Discovery Park
Lucky Peak Reservoir
Crow Inn
Diversion Dam (Parking)
Eckert Road (Parking)
21
River
S
2,720'
Municipal Park (Parking)
Golf Course
Springs Ave
Warm
Walnut
Boise
Blvd
Avenue
Park Center
Boise
Elevation
10000
8750
7500
6250
5000
3750
2500
0
2
4
6
8
Mileage
1 mile

RECOMMENDED SIDE TRIPS

For cyclists who are just starting to work up a sweat and want to ride farther, we suggest the following possibilities:

■Ride the dirt back to Boise on the old Oregon Trail. See Page 29 for ride description and map.

■Ride Idaho 21 to Highland Valley Summit. It's about 3.8 miles and 900 vertical feet from Discovery Park to the summit.

■Ride Idaho 21 to Highland Valley Road, climb 3,300 vertical feet to Lucky Peak and ride dirt jeep trails back to Boise. This is an expert loop for people who like to climb. See Page 83 for ride description and map.

■Ride Idaho 21 east to Robie Creek Road, turn left, and ride back over Aldape Summit via Rocky Canyon Road to Boise. Riders who attempt this loop should start early in the day. This loop is harder than the Oregon Trail loop and easier than the climb over Lucky Peak.

BEGINNER OFF-PAVEMENT RIDES

OREGON TRAIL-GREENBELT LOOP

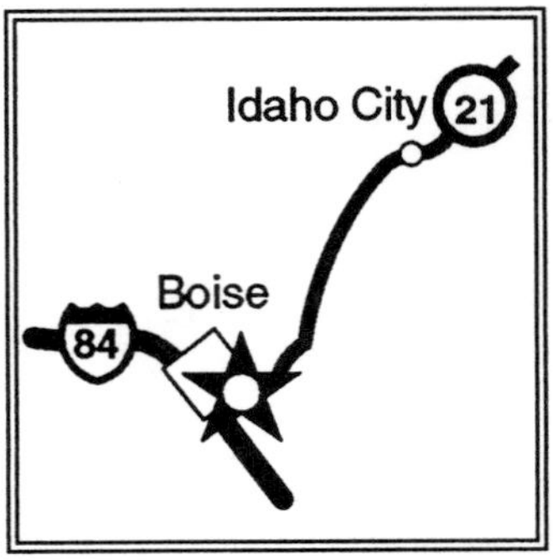

Quality: ***
Distance: 18.5 miles
Difficulty: Advanced beginner
Riding time: 1.5-3.5 hours
Trail: 4WD road, paved path
Season: Year-round, weather permitting
Caution: Yield to construction crews
Topo: Boise South

Getting there: Ride the Greenbelt (either side) or drive to the junction of Eckert Road and Boise Avenue. Follow Eckert (south) up the hill, where it turns into Amity. Follow Amity to Holcomb St., turn left and ride to the "Oregon Trail" subdivision. As you approach the hill, note the old wagon tracks cutting down the bench behind the homes. On top of the hill, it turns into Eastgate Street. Follow Eastgate to Mimosa, turn right and jump on the bike path running through Columbia Village, heading east toward Lucky Peak (go left). If you're driving to the start, this is a good place to start riding.

The Ride: Eventually, Columbia Village will be developed such that the neighborhood bike path runs for several miles to the east to a new Idaho 21 spur from I-84. Highway Department plans call for a bike path to run alongside the Idaho 21 spur and intersect with the Greenbelt. At the time of our publication, the Oregon Trail could be reached by following the Columbia Village bike path to a temporary dead end, turn right and head southeast for the upper bench. Two jeep trails climb up to the next bench, where the Oregon Trail route begins. One is above the sports complex; the other climbs the bench underneath a triple-pole powerline. Take your pick and follow the jeep trail in an easterly direction toward Lucky Peak. The trail follows the rim overlooking the Boise River. Several jeep trails traverse the bench; we recommend the two-track trail that cuts closest to the rim, offering the best view. At 3.8 miles the trail intersects a gravel road about 300 yards from a tree-bordered ranch; go left and then left again back on the Oregon Trail. At mile 5, within sight of Lucky Peak Dam, the trail bends right; stay with it for 8/10ths of a mile to a T-junction. Go left and notice the old Oregon Trail ruts leading to Bonneville Point straight ahead. Take the left branch at the next three junctions and follow the low road to Lucky Peak Dam and Turner Gulch. At 7.85 miles is a T-junction, turn left to head toward the dam. In another 2/10ths is a junction with the Turner Gulch Road, go left and head for Discovery Park. Cyclists can either ride the pavement for a screaming descent down Idaho 21 or drop down toward the power plant on a dirt road that leads to the beach and the park. You've come 10 miles from Boise. **In Discovery Park,** pick up the Greenbelt and cruise back to Boise. It's 8.5 miles to Municipal Park.
Interpretive remarks: Thousands of emigrants crossed the Oregon Trail through Boise from the 1860s to the 1880s. After a 1,500-mile, strenuous journey through the hot, dusty desert, the Boise River Valley was, indeed, a welcome sight. Lucky Peak Dam was constructed in 1958 as a flood-control, irrigation and recreation project.

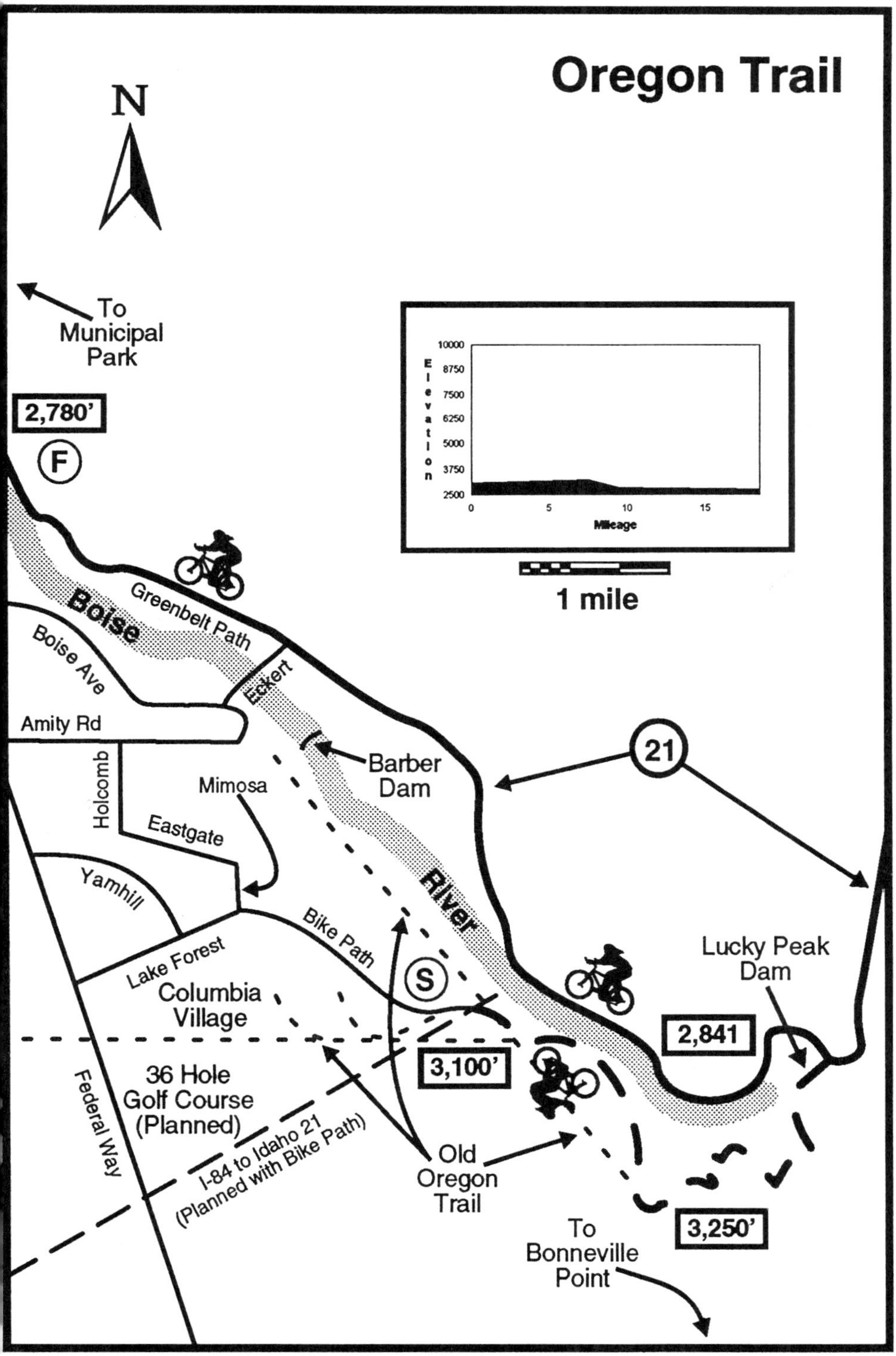
Oregon Trail
N
To Municipal Park
2,780'
F
10000
8750
7500
6250
5000
3750
2500
Elevation
0
5
10
15
Mileage
1 mile
Boise
Greenbelt Path
Boise Ave
Amity Rd
Eckert
Barber Dam
21
Holcomb
Mimosa
Eastgate
River
Yamhill
Bike Path
Lake Forest
S
Columbia Village
Lucky Peak Dam
2,841
3,100'
36 Hole Golf Course (Planned)
Federal Way
I-84 to Idaho 21 (Planned with Bike Path)
Old Oregon Trail
3,250'
To Bonneville Point

BOGUS BASIN BEGINNER LOOP

Quality: ***
Distance: 4.5 miles
Difficulty: Beginner
Riding time: 1-1.5
Trail: 2WD road, single-track trail
Season: May-October
Topo map: Shafer Butte
Watch out for: Occasional motorcycles on the trail.

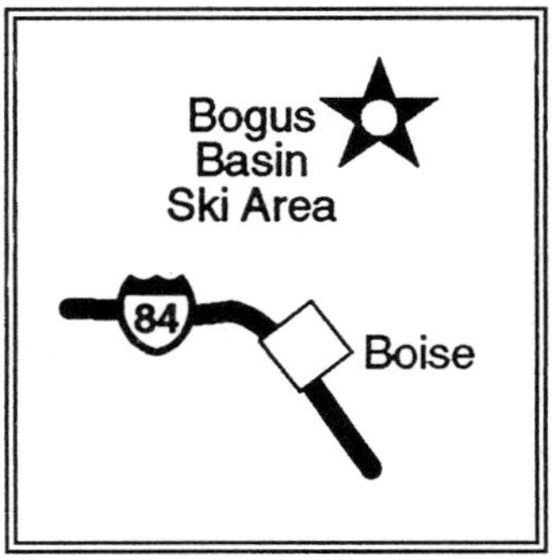

Getting there: From Boise, drive north on Bogus Basin Road 16 miles to the lower lodge parking lot. Once the road turns to dirt, you're on the Boise Ridge Road. Follow the dirt road past the ski area about 3.3 miles to a junction on the right to the Shafer Butte Picnic Area. Park; the ride starts here.

The Ride: Ride 1.23 miles up to the Shafer Butte picnic area to a fork, go left. At 1.29 miles, turn left just past the Mores Mountain paved interpretive trail. After about 40 yards, bear left on single-track trail to a junction of two trails. Stay on the right-hand trail and pedal into the trees. This single-track trail is mostly downhill. Proceed with caution -- watch for sudden dips in the trail. At 2.9 total miles, the trail exits on the Boise Ridge Road. Turn left and ride back to your rig. The road rises about a half-mile and then it's all downhill to the vehicle.

Interpretive remarks: In June and July, wildflowers create a rainbow of colors on the landscape. In the fall, cyclists will enjoy the bright variety of colors on shrubs and trees -- brilliant reds, yellows and greens across the mountains. Riders will notice impressive granite rocks rising from the earth on Mores Mountain. These are typical features of the Idaho Batholith, a massive granitic geological formation that begins to the north of Boise and extends north beyond the Salmon River.

Combo activities: Wildflower identification, camping, picnic lunch at the picnic area, rock climbing on granite spires.

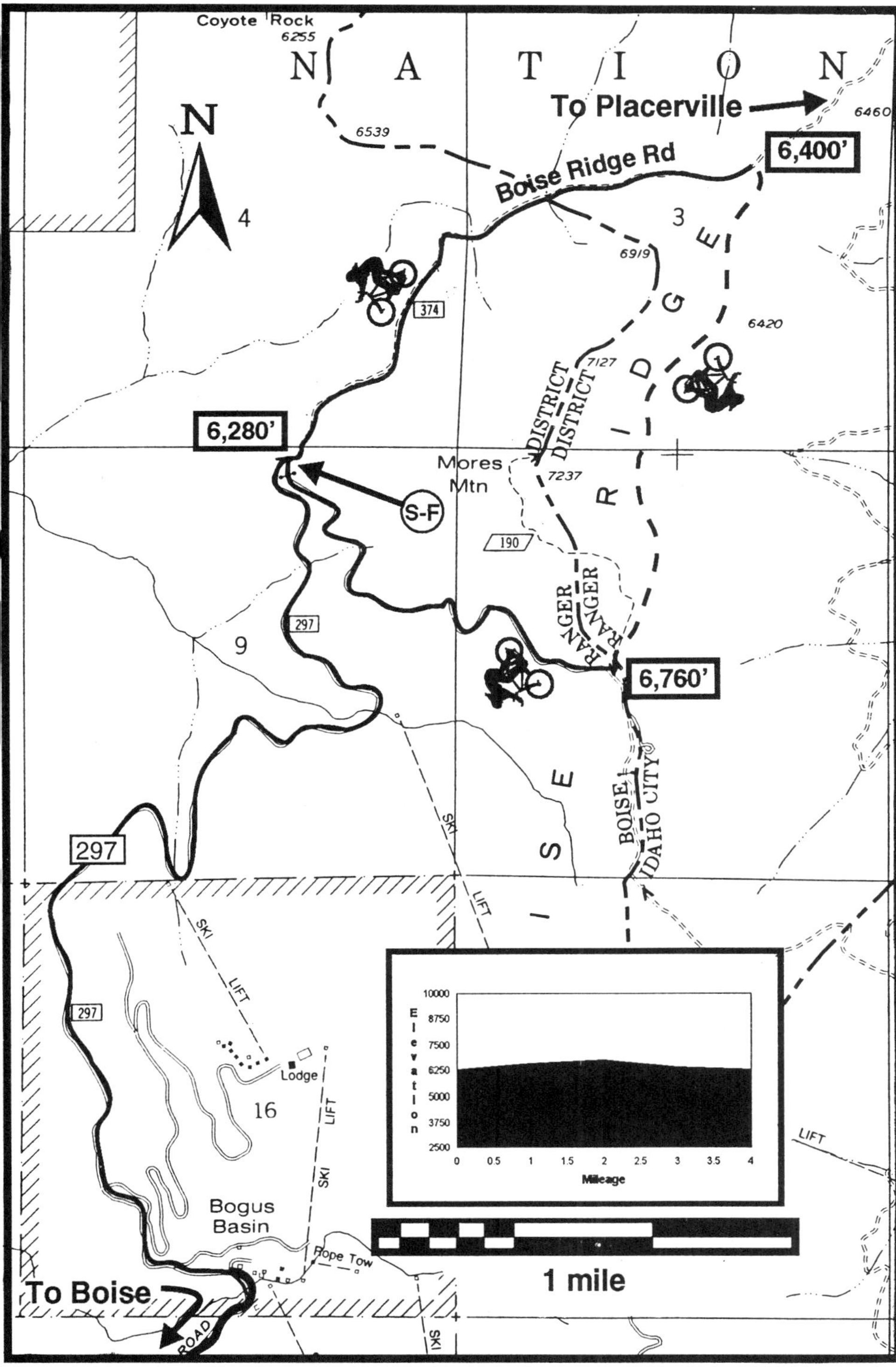
Coyote Rock
6255
N A T I O N
To Placerville
6460
6539
Boise Ridge Rd
6,400'
N
4
3
6919
374
6420
7127
DISTRICT
DISTRICT
R I D G E
6,280'
Mores Mtn
7237
S-F
190
RANGER
RANGER
297
9
6,760'
BOISE
IDAHO CITY
S E
SKI
LIFT
297
297
Lodge
16
Bogus Basin
Rope Tow
To Boise
ROAD
Elevation
Mileage
1 mile

NORTH FORK OF THE BOISE RIVER

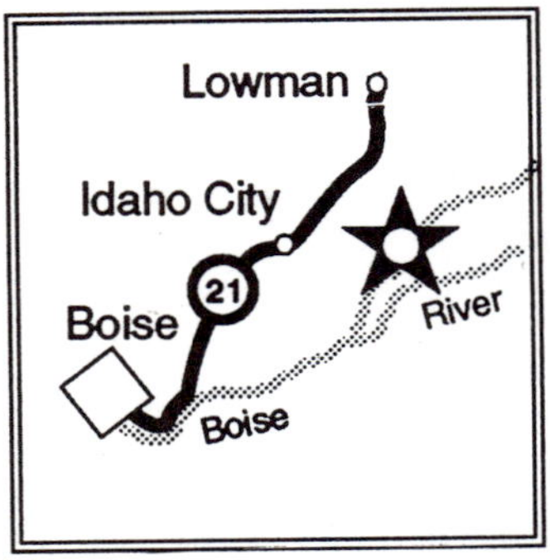

Quality: **
Distance: 1-30 miles
Difficulty: beginner
Riding time: You make the call
Trail: 2WD dirt road
Season: May-October
Watch out for: traffic, logging trucks

Getting there: From Boise, drive east on Idaho 21 about 47 miles, just past Idaho City, to the Granite Creek-Rabbit Creek Road (USFS Road No. 327). Turn right and follow the road about 14 miles to the North Fork of the Boise River.

The Ride: Find a place to pull over along the North Fork Road, unload the bikes and go for a ride. From Black Rock campground, the North Fork Road continues for 17 miles to Deer Park. It's a 2WD dirt road, which gets narrow in places, but it's a gentle grade for the whole distance (average gain of 45 feet per mile). This is the ultimate place for a family ride -- a beautiful mountain setting, an easy grade and a decent road surface. Many dirt roads splinter off the main road on the way to Deer Park (see below for recommended side trips). On weekends, parents should keep their children close and watch out for vehicles or motorcycles speeding down the road out of control. The traffic is likely to be lighter between Barber Flat and Deer Park. How far you go and where you go is totally up to you and your ability.

We heartily recommend that families and other cyclists consider camping along the river for a night or two. Jillions of prime car-camping sites are located along the North Fork. Besides mountain biking, there are many other activities to enjoy.

Recommended side trips:
-- **Barber Flat to Alexander Flats.** 7 miles, one way. Ride over a 1,000-foot divide to the Middle Fork of the Boise River. (See Middle Fork ride for side trips)
-- **Hungarian Creek Road.** Six miles of logging road to a dead end, 6 miles back.
-- **Big Owl Creek Road.** The turnoff is right before the Edna Creek Road (USFS Road No. 384).
-- **Trapper Creek-Grand Mountain loop.** (Expert ride; see detailed ride and map, Page 77.)
-- **Willow Creek-Crooked River-Hunter Creek loop.** Park at the Willow Creek campground along the Edna Creek Road. It's about 6 miles east of Idaho 21. Ride on USFS Road No. 348 for about 16 miles to Deer Park. It's a 2WD road the whole way with several gradual uphills and long downhills. Rated excellent for intermediate riders.
-- **Deer Park to Dutch Creek.** 10 miles, one way. Ride over an 800-foot divide to the Middle Fork of the Boise River on USFS Road No. 327. At the junction with the Middle Fork, the road continues south to the Trinity Lakes (gonzo riders, it's only 20 miles!).

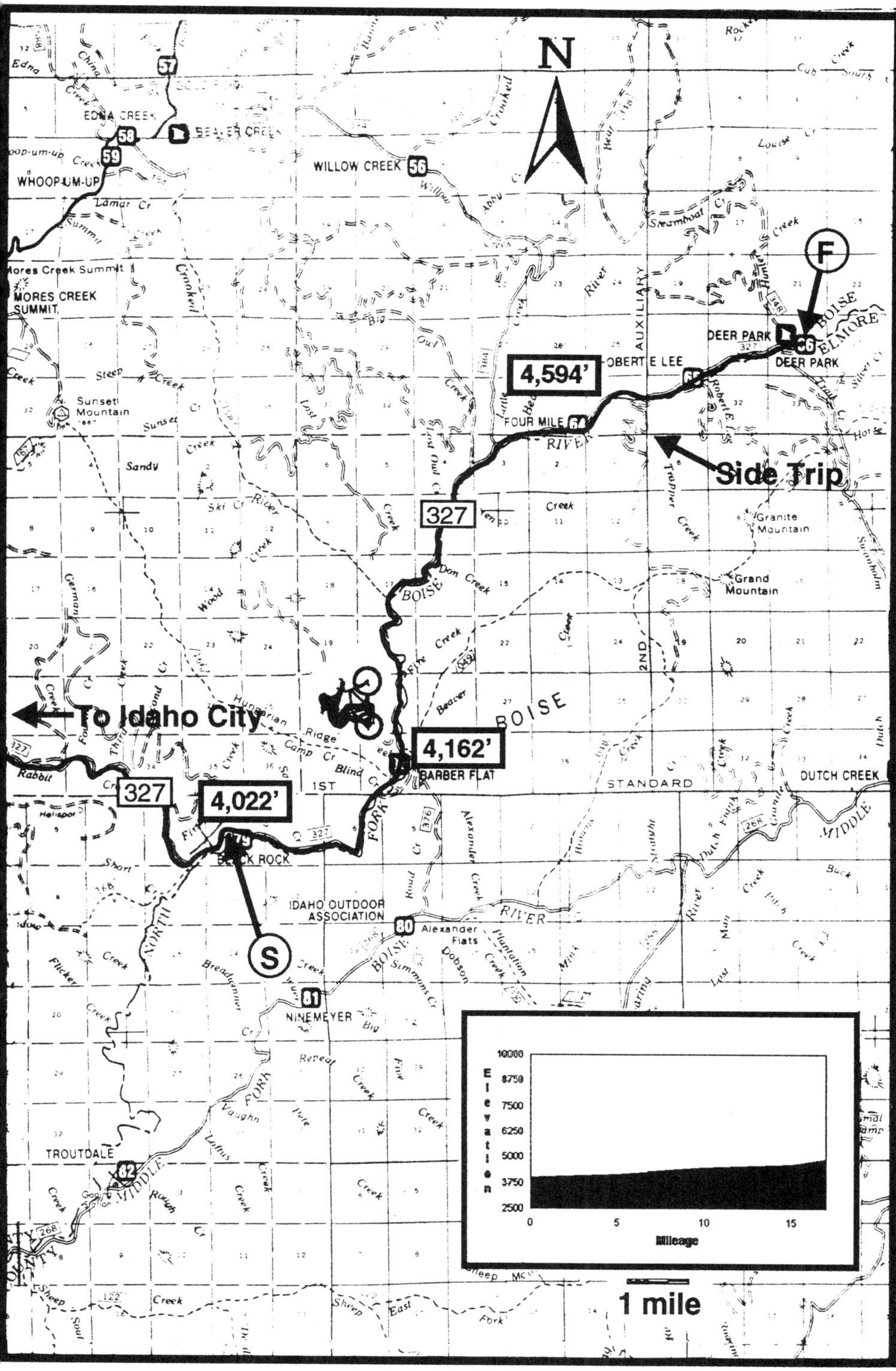
N
EDNA CREEK
BEAVER CREEK
WHOOP-UM-UP
WILLOW CREEK
Mores Creek Summit
MORES CREEK SUMMIT
Sunset Mountain
DEER PARK
ELMORE
BOISE
ROBERT E LEE
4,594'
FOUR MILE
RIVER
AUXILIARY
Side Trip
327
Granite Mountain
Grand Mountain
Don Creek
BOISE
2ND
To Idaho City
4,162'
BARBER FLAT
STANDARD
DUTCH CREEK
1ST
327
4,022'
BLACK ROCK
MIDDLE
NORTH
IDAHO OUTDOOR ASSOCIATION
Alexander Flats
RIVER
NINEMEYER
TROUTDALE
F
S
Elevation
10000
8750
7500
6250
5000
3750
2500
0
5
10
15
Mileage
1 mile

MIDDLE FORK PAYETTE RIVER

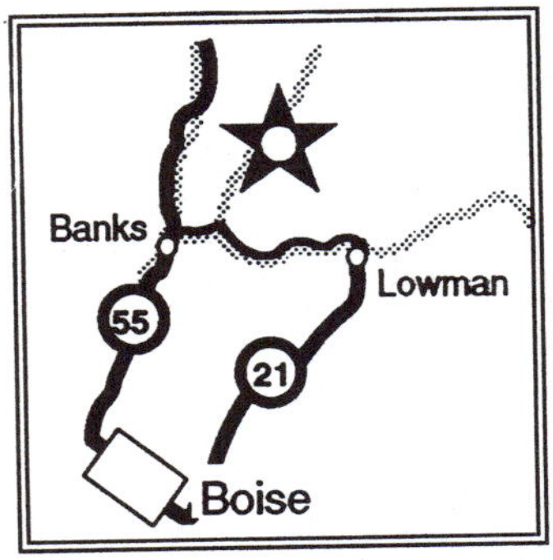

Quality: **
Distance: 1-15 miles
Difficulty: beginner
Riding time: You make the call
Trail: 2WD dirt road
Season: May-October
Watch out for: ATVs, vehicle traffic, logging trucks

Getting there: From Boise, drive north on Idaho 55 about 34 miles to Banks. Cross the bridge, turn right and drive about eight miles to the Crouch turnoff; turn left. Go about eight miles north of Crouch to the Tie Creek Campground; this marks the beginning of Boise National Forest land (public land). Cyclists can begin riding here or from points to the north.

The Ride: A wide, 2WD dirt road traverses the Middle Fork of the Payette River for about 15 miles from Tie Creek Campground to Boiling Springs Campground. In between, there are three campgrounds (Hardscrabble, Rattlesnake and Trail Creek), where you could make a base camp. Beginners could get a feel for riding off the pavement by riding along the road and enjoying the views and the pine-scented air. Look for old logging roads taking off to the right or left from the main road to practice riding uphill and get away from the traffic. The traffic is not as heavy if you turn right 16.5 miles north of Crouch toward the Silver Creek Plunge. The curvy road goes over a small summit and falls into the Silver Creek area, where there are numerous unmarked camping areas north of the plunge. The Plunge is a resort that has a hot springs pool and many camping areas as well; it charges a small camping and swimming fee.
Remember: On weekends, parents should keep their children close and watch out for vehicles or motorcycles speeding down the road out of control. How far you go and where you go is totally up to you and your ability.

We heartily recommend that families and other cyclists consider camping along the river for a night or two. Many prime car-camping sites are located along the Middle Fork and Silver Creek. Besides mountain biking, there are many other activities to enjoy.

Recommended side trips:
-- **Six-Mile Creek:** USFS Road No. 670 takes off to the left from the main Middle Fork road and climbs abruptly to a forested ridge overlooking Round Valley. Strong riders could ride this road and drop over to Smith's Ferry; but you'll need someone to pick you up.
-- **West Fork:** USFS Road No. 300 takes off to the left from the main Middle Fork road and climbs quickly to the ridgetop. Eventually, the road, or a single-track trail, goes to East Mountain.

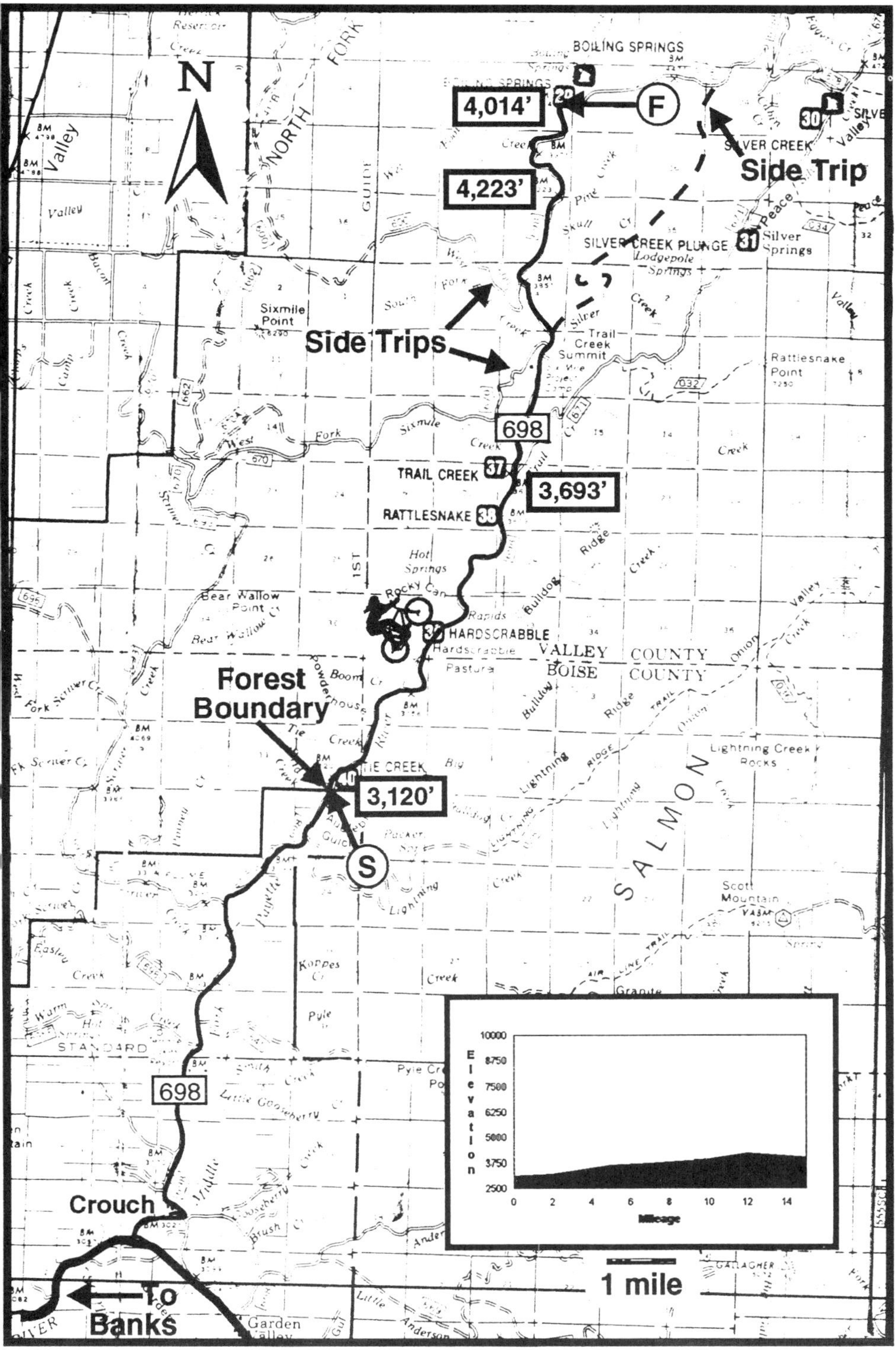
N
BOILING SPRINGS
4,014'
F
Side Trip
SILVER CREEK
4,223'
SILVER CREEK PLUNGE
Silver Springs
Sixmile Point
Side Trips
Trail Creek Summit
Rattlesnake Point
698
TRAIL CREEK
3,693'
RATTLESNAKE
Hot Springs
Bear Wallow Point
HARDSCRABBLE
VALLEY COUNTY
BOISE COUNTY
Forest Boundary
TIE CREEK
3,120'
S
SALMON
Lightning Creek Rocks
Scott Mountain
STANDARD
698
Crouch
To Banks
Garden Valley
1 mile
Elevation
10000
8750
7500
6250
5000
3750
2500
0
2
4
6
8
10
12
14
Mileage

SILVER CITY BEGINNER RIDE

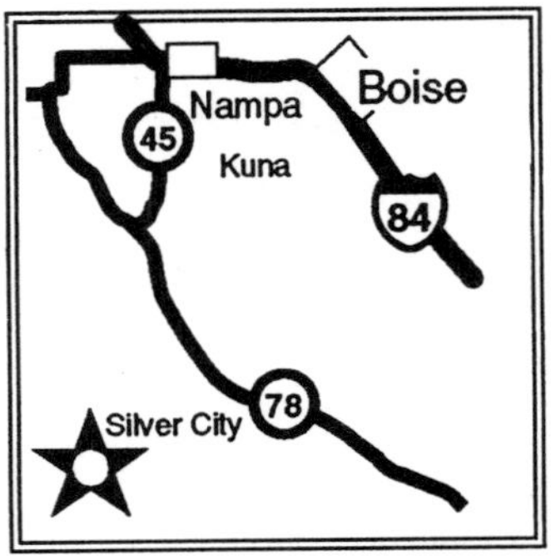

Quality: ***
Distance: 6 miles round-trip
Difficulty: Beginner
Riding time: 1 hour or more
Trail: 4WD dirt road
Season: May-October
Caution: Watch out for other trail users
Topo map: Silver City

Getting there: Drive to downtown Nampa and take Idaho 45 south toward Melba. Stay on Idaho 45 until you reach a junction with Idaho 78, go left toward Murphy. Proceed through Murphy and it's four miles to the Silver City turnoff on the right. The turn is marked, and it's 19 miles of bumpy, washboard-ridden dirt road to the quaint, old mining town nestled in a high basin of the Owyhee Mountains at 6,300 feet. Drive over the New York Summit to a junction marked by a permanent outhouse at 18 miles. Turn left and drive about a mile through town to an undeveloped campground. Park. The ride starts here.

About the ride: Follow a 4WD dirt road that starts from the campground and runs along Jordan Creek for 2.3 miles. Ignore sketchy two-track roads heading off the main road (unless you want to explore a little bit for fun) and ride along the creek. The road crosses the creek several times; the creek-crossings are rideable during periods of low runoff. At 2.3 miles, the jeep trail bends to the right and starts climbing abruptly. Those who want an extra workout can follow the road a half-mile farther to a junction with a two-track jeep trail on the left. Turn left at 2.8 miles and follow the jeep trail for two-tenths of a mile to a dead-end in a small meadow. This is the end of the route, and it's a good lunch spot, offering views of the headwaters of Jordan Creek. Return as you came.

Interpretive remarks: Jordan Creek is named after Michael Jordan, who along with W.T. Carson, led 29 men from the Idaho City area to the Owyhees and struck gold in the creek in 1863. Silver City became the county seat in 1866 as other gold and silver discoveries brought several thousand miners to the area. However, the territory was still controlled by Shoshone-Paiute Indians, and Jordan was killed by the Indians the following year. Behind the mountains rimming Silver City, the NORANDA Mining Co. operates a large open-pit gold and silver mine named after Capt. Joseph R. DeLamar, who first discovered the massive mineral deposit in 1863. The county seat was later moved to Murphy.

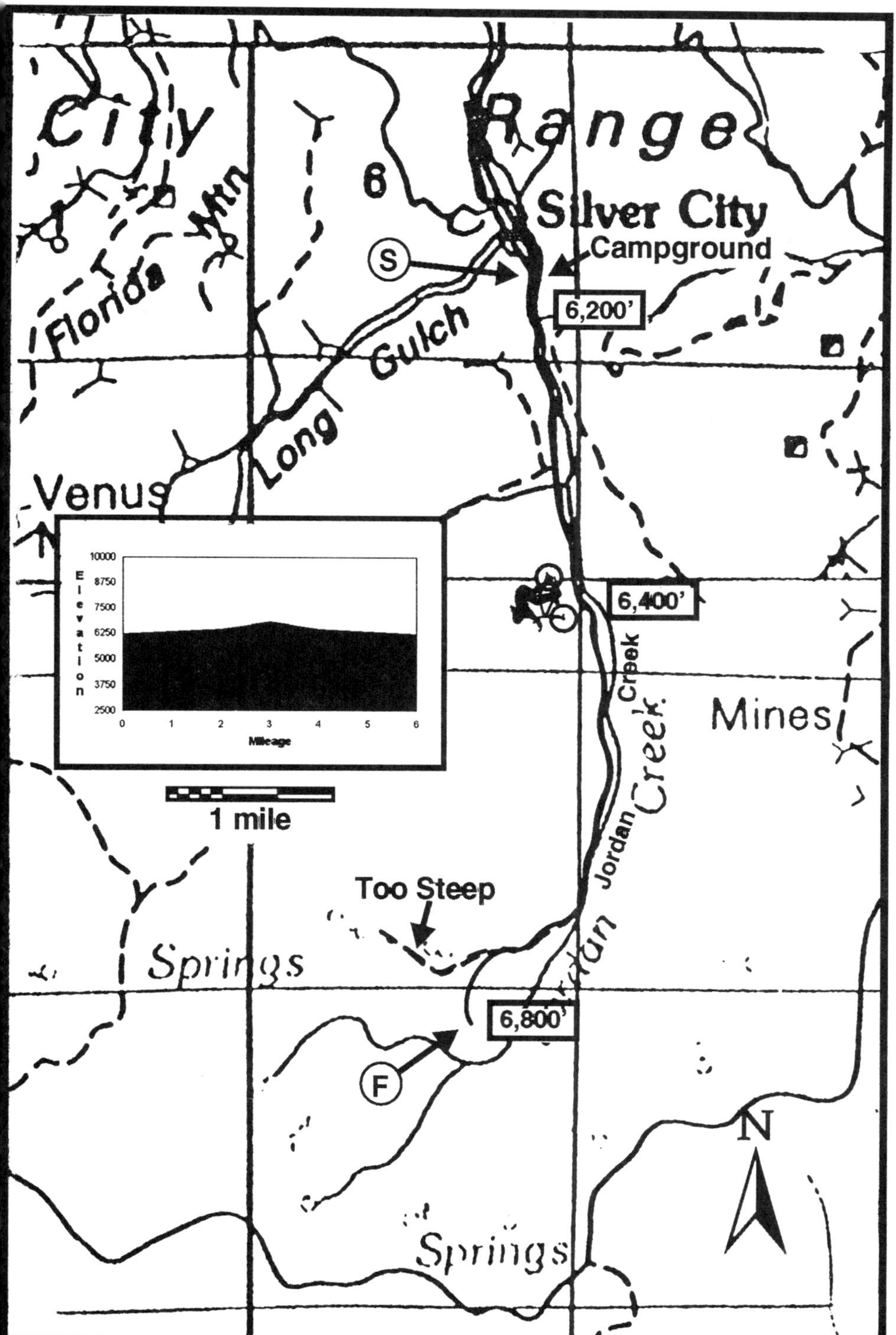
City
Range
6
Silver City
Campground
S
6,200'
Florida Mtn
Long Gulch
Venus
6,400'
Jordan Creek
Creek
Mines
1 mile
Too Steep
Springs
6,800'
F
N
Springs
Elevation
10000
8750
7500
6250
5000
3750
2500
0
1
2
3
4
5
6
Mileage

SWAN FALLS NORTH-SIDE LOOP

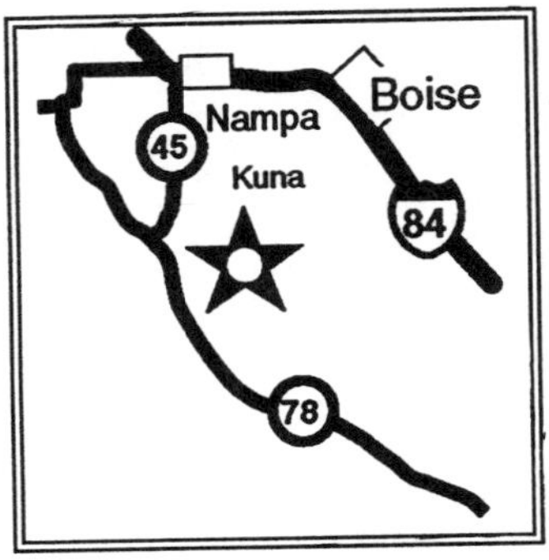

Quality: ***
Distance: 17.26 miles
Difficulty: Beginner
Riding time: 1.5-4 hours
Trail: 4WD dirt road, single-track trail
Season: Year-round, depending on weather
Cautions: Heavy multiple-use area

Getting there: Take I-84 to the Meridian exit; turn left and head for Kuna (about 10 miles). On the east end of downtown Kuna, watch for a sign to the Snake River Birds of Prey Area. Turn left and head 18 miles for Swan Falls Dam. A steep switchback takes you to the bottom of the canyon; park to the west (downstream) of the dam.

The Ride: The Swan Falls loop follows mostly 4WD road on relatively flat terrain along the north side of the Snake River canyon, downstream from the dam. Watch for hawks, eagles, falcons and owls -- the canyon is home to the densest-known nesting population of birds of prey, some 250 pairs. Depending on the time of year, this ride offers varying degrees of obstacles -- ruts, rocks and sands. Proceed with caution. Follow the 4WD dirt road heading west about 150 yards to the first junction; turn right. Continue for 600-700 yards and rejoin the main road. At 5.4 miles, take the right-hand fork and follow the road along the base of the cliff. At 8.3 miles, you will reach Lake Halverson, a good lunch spot. From the western end of the lake, climb up a small ridge on a single-track trail that winds through boulders and brush. The trail descends back to the river. If you have trouble finding the trail, follow the road in an easterly direction about 1 mile to the east until you arrive at a rock bivouac site and stone cabin built by Chinese laborers around the turn of the century. Take a second to check it out. Proceed back toward the dam by riding north across the canyon flat to the main 4WD dirt road. Turn right and return the way you came.

Interpretive remarks: The Snake River canyon was formed by the Bonneville Flood (circa 13,000 B.C.). Floodwaters rushed through the canyon carrying water from Lake Idaho, which spanned from the Snake River Plain from American Falls to Weiser. On its crashing route, it carved the canyon observed today and deposited boulders in the canyon floor.

Variations: Take your bike across the walkway on the dam face and ride the single-track and 4WD road on the north side of the river to Walter's Ferry (about 20 miles one-way). Cross the old bridge, and ride back to the dam on the north side of the river.

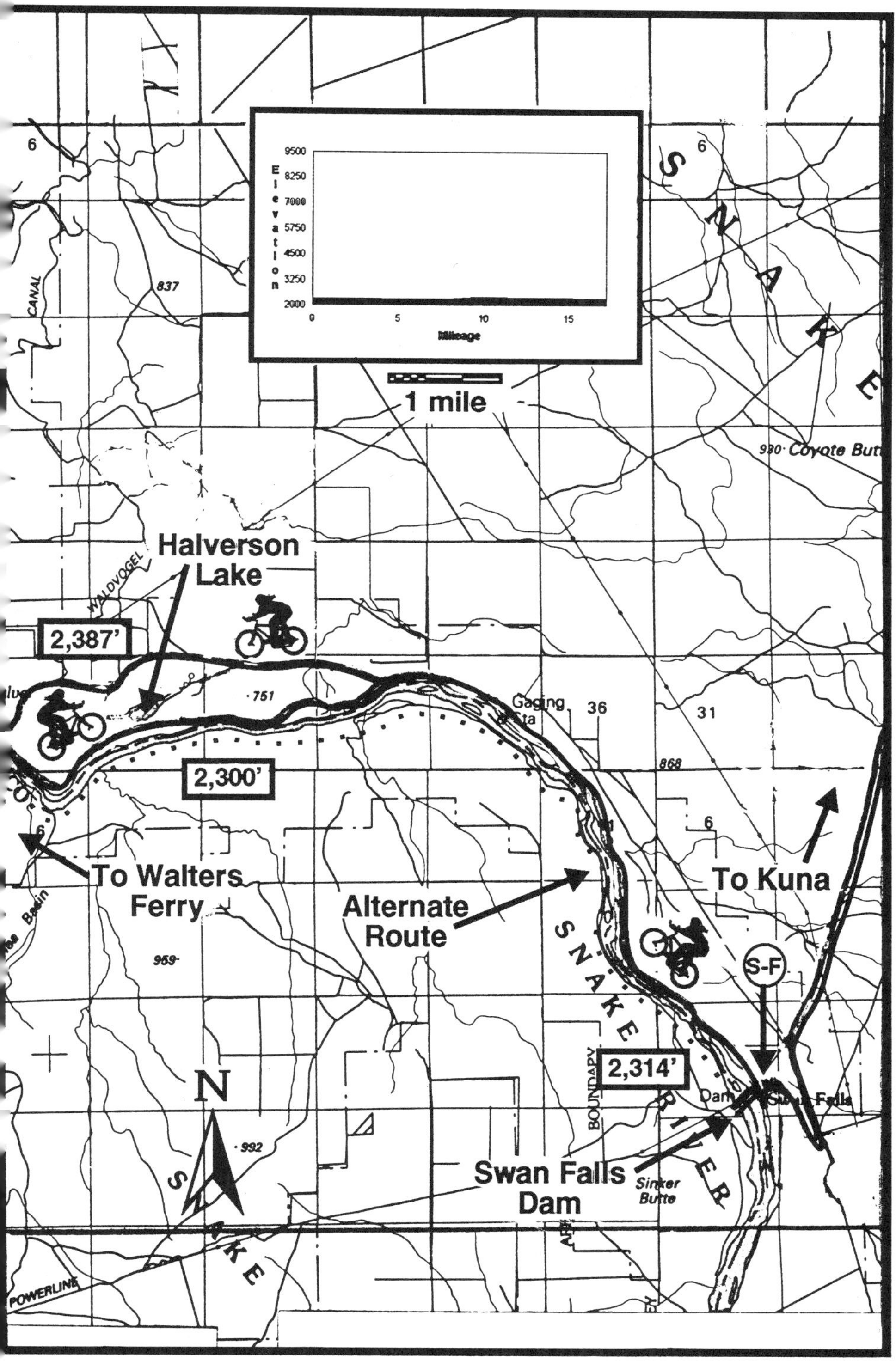
Elevation
9500
8250
7000
5750
4500
3250
2000
0
5
10
15
Mileage
1 mile
SNAKE
6
837
CANAL
930 Coyote Butte
Halverson Lake
WALDVOGEL
2,387'
751
Gaging Sta
36
31
868
2,300'
6
To Walters Ferry
Alternate Route
To Kuna
SNAKE RIVER
S-F
959
BOUNDARY
2,314'
Dam
Swan Falls
N
992
Swan Falls Dam
Sinker Butte
SNAKE
POWERLINE

LESLIE GULCH

Quality: ***
Distance: 1-5 miles
Difficulty: Beginner
Riding time: You make the call
Season: March-November
Trail: 2WD, 4WD dirt road
Topo map: Rooster Comb

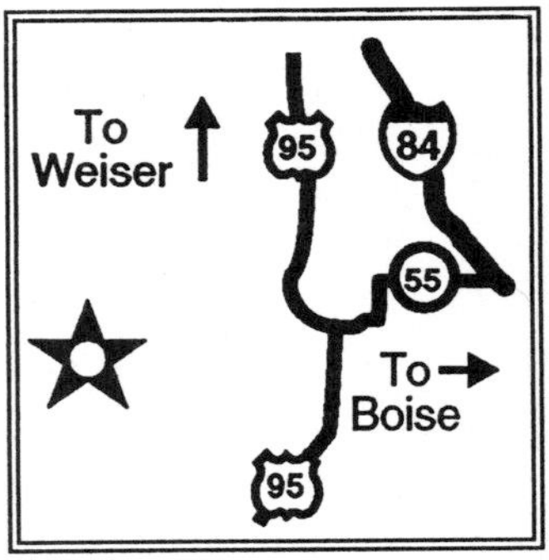

Getting there: From Boise, take I-84 to Nampa and take the exit in front of the Amalgamated Sugar Factory. Turn right and proceed to the stop sign in front of the factory. Turn left and follow the road to the first stop light. Go straight. Now you're on Idaho Highway 55 heading west for Marsing. The road goes by the St. Chapelle Winery, if you want to take time for a tour. Just past Marsing, Idaho 55 intersects with U.S. 95, turn left on U.S. 95 and head south about 10 miles until you see a sign for Leslie Gulch on the right-hand side of the road. Turn right and follow the signs. It's about 24 miles of dirt road to the area. Drive over the summit into the gulch to a wooden cabin; parking is available about 100 yards down the road on the right-hand side. This is also the trailhead for Juniper Gulch (walking path only).

The Ride: Leslie Gulch does not offer extensive areas for mountain biking, but enough to give visitors an overview of the magnificent rock formations. As you drive over a summit and drop into the gulch, red-streaked monoliths, spires and arches rise magically from the non-descript sagebrush desert. Turkey vultures and red-tailed hawks circle above, chukar partridges chatter on the mountainside, and bighorn sheep slowly graze the tall, thick bunchgrass slopes. From the parking area, ride downhill about 4 miles to Owyhee Reservoir. Hiking opportunties abound on either side of the road. On your way back, ride past the parking area to the cabin, and turn right up Dago Gulch. This two-track road proceeds up Dago Gulch for about a mile to a locked gate indicating the beginning of private land. Turn around and head back to your vehicle.

Interpretive remarks: Painted rocks in Leslie Gulch are called tuffs, formed by rhyolite ash flows up to 1,000 feet thick, according to the Bureau of Land Management. Volcanic eruptions from nearby Mahogany Mountain deposited the tuffs, which were shaped over time by wind and water. Seventeen California bighorn sheep were introduced to Leslie Gulch in 1965. Since then, the herd has expanded to about 200 wild sheep. The best times for seeing the sheep are in the early morning or evening. Leslie Gulch is named after Hiram E. Leslie, who was struck and killed by lightning in 1882 while working his cattle.

Combo activities: We recommend that cyclists bring their camping gear to Leslie Gulch and spend the weekend riding, hiking and exploring the scenic area. The best primitive camping areas are in Dago Gulch. Bring lots of potable water with you.

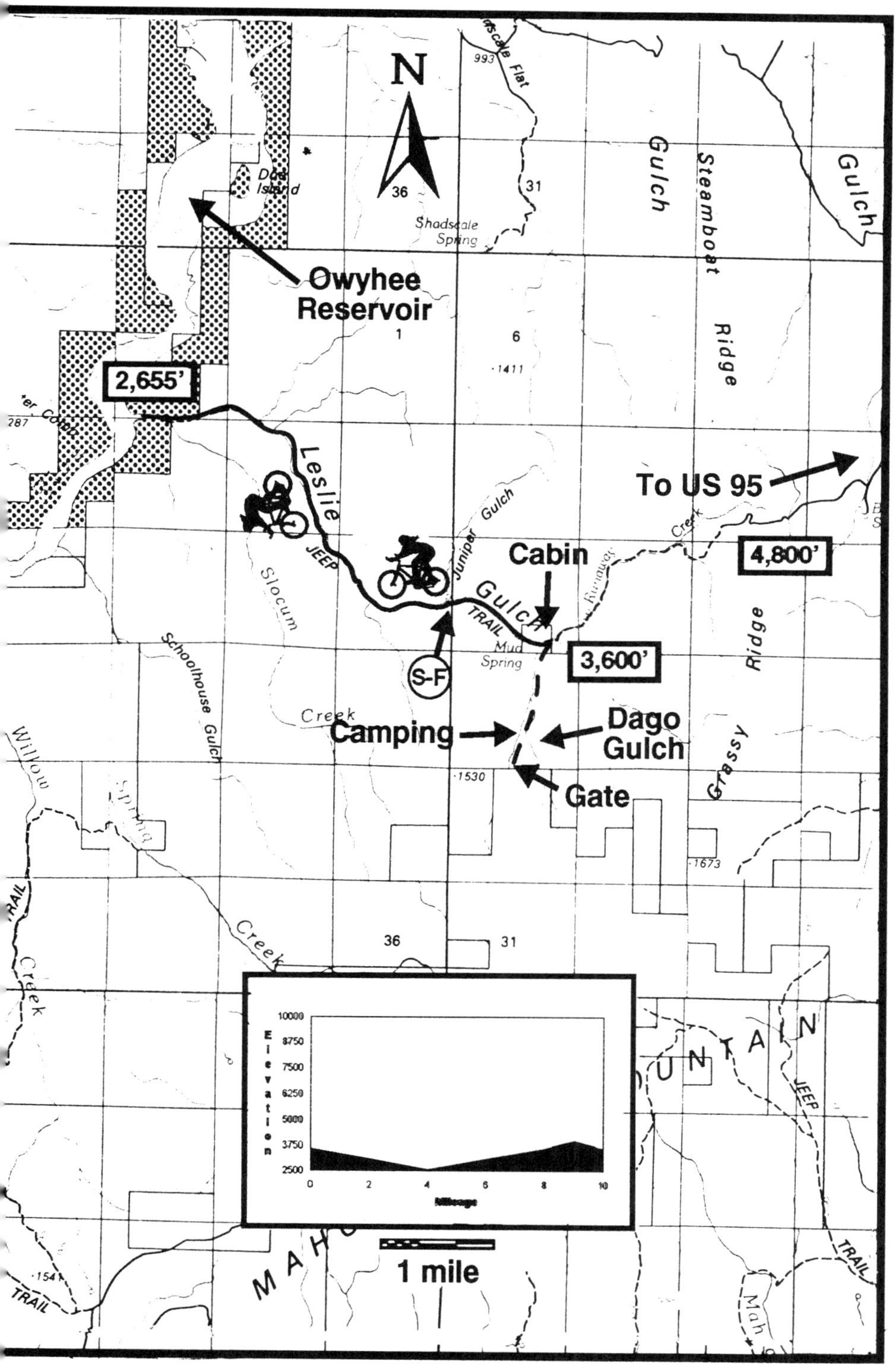
N
Owyhee Reservoir
Doe Island
Shadscale Spring
Shadscale Flat
Gulch
Steamboat Ridge
Gulch
2,655'
Leslie Gulch
JEEP TRAIL
Juniper Gulch
To US 95
Cabin
4,800'
Runaway Creek
Slocum Creek
Schoolhouse Gulch
Mud Spring
3,600'
S-F
Camping
Dago Gulch
Gate
Grassy Ridge
Willow Creek
Spring Creek
Creek
36
31
1
6
1411
1530
1673
993
MAHOGANY MOUNTAIN
JEEP
TRAIL
Elevation
10000
8750
7500
6250
5000
3750
2500
0
2
4
6
8
10
Mileage
1 mile

DEADWOOD RIVER SCENIC TOUR

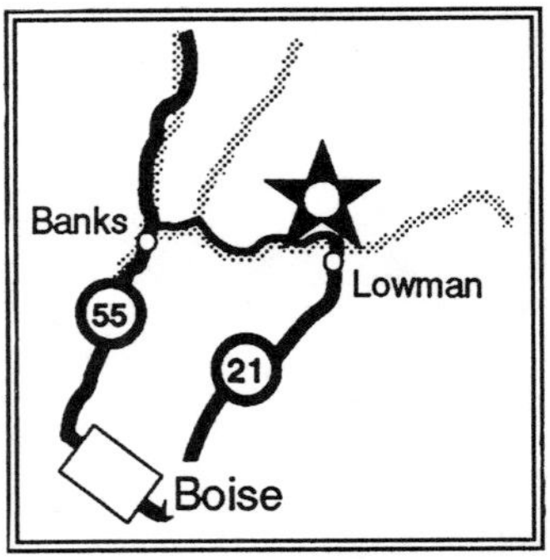

Quality: ***
Distance: 14 miles (7 one-way)
Difficulty: Beginner
Riding time: 1.5-3 hours
Trail: 2WD dirt road
Season: May-October
Topos: Pine Flats, Scott Creek

Getting there: From Boise, drive north on Idaho 55 for 34 miles to Banks. Cross the bridge over the South Fork Payette River and turn right. Proceed on the Banks-Lowman Road for about 30 miles to the Deadwood Campground on the left-hand side of the road. The campground is about seven miles west of Lowman. Park. The ride starts here.

The Ride: This is our favorite up-and-back scenic ride for beginning mountain bikers and families in the guidebook. The ride features a gentle grade, very little vehicular traffic and pleasant views of the Deadwood River. If 14 miles seems too far, beginners can ride as far as they wish, turn around and head back. Start the ride by turning right out of the campground on the highway, cross the bridge over the Deadwood River, and then turn right on USFS Road #024GB. There is a sign for Julie Creek trailhead at the turnoff. The road starts out fairly flat and begins to rise at a reasonable grade for several miles. Enjoy the views overlooking the winding river, beaver ponds in oxbows, and the mixed ponderosa pine-Douglas fir forest. At about 4 miles, cyclists climb toward a small summit on the road at 5.5 miles. From there, the road descends for 1.5 miles to the Julie Creek trailhead. An undeveloped campground borders the river at this point, and a handicapped access outhouse is located here as well. This is an excellent spot for lunch. Return as you came.

Combo activities: Stronger riders could carry their fishing pole along with a lunch and do some fishing while the rest of the group or family catches up. Riders also could take a short hike up the Julie Creek Trail. Others: camping, swimming, whitewater boating, mushroom picking, wildflower identification, photography. Caution: families should not tube the Deadwood River. It is an expert-only Class V whitewater run and contains numerous "strainers" -- trees fallen over in the stream, which can pin boats or people in strong currents.

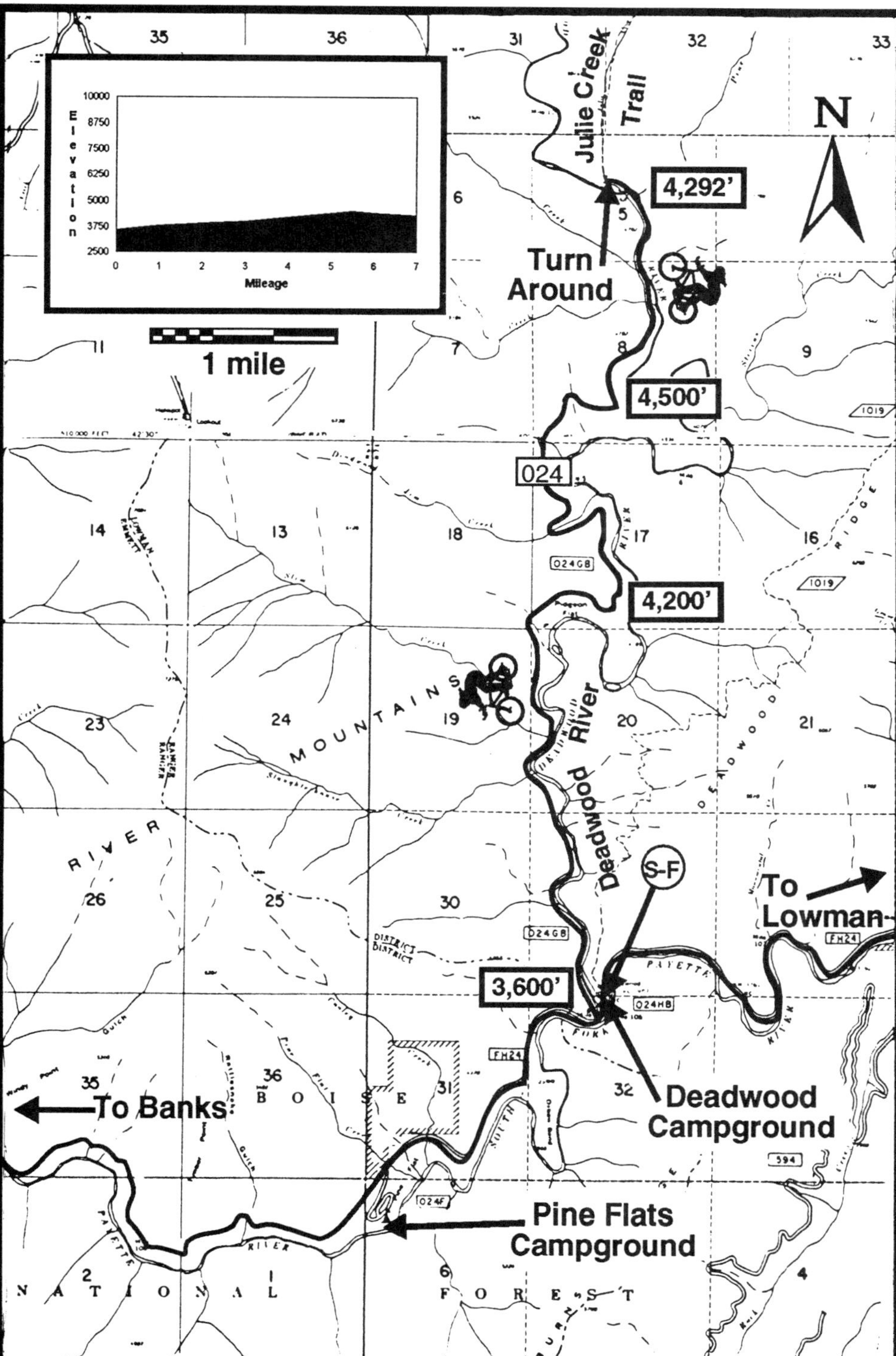
Julie Creek Trail
N
4,292'
Turn Around
4,500'
024
4,200'
Deadwood River
MOUNTAINS
S-F
To Lowman
3,600'
Deadwood Campground
To Banks
BOISE
Pine Flats Campground
NATIONAL FOREST
1 mile
Elevation
Mileage
10000
8750
7500
6250
5000
3750
2500
0
1
2
3
4
5
6
7

SILVER CREEK LOOKOUT

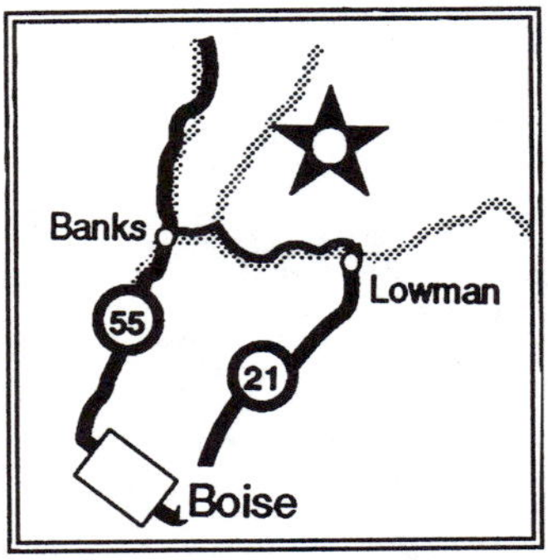

Quality: ***
Distance: 2.5 miles; 5 miles roundtrip
Difficulty: beginner/intermediate
Riding time: 20-45 minutes to the lookout
Trail: 2WD dirt road
Season: late May-October
Watch out for: vehicles, ATVs
Topo: Boiling Springs

Getting there: From Boise, drive north on Idaho 55 about 34 miles to Banks. Cross the bridge, turn right and drive about eight miles to the Crouch turnoff; turn left. Go 24 miles north to the junction with USFS Road #678 (just before Boiling Springs Campground), turn right. Proceed 4 miles to the junction with a dirt road leading to the Silver Creek Lookout (USFS Road #678B). Park. The ride starts here.

The ride: Follow the 2WD dirt road toward the lookout. At seven-tenths of a mile, an old logging road peels off to the left; ambitious riders could explore the road as a side trip; others should stay on the main road. The 2.5-mile route winds through Douglas fir and ponderosa pine forests to the lookout. The vertical gain is 1,218 feet, or about 490 feet per mile. Most cyclists should be able to ride the grade in low gear. Near the top, watch out for the Forest Service gate. It is open 9 a.m. to 6 p.m. to reduce vandalism and protect the privacy of the lookout personnel. On top, the 360-degree view at 6,778 feet is spectacular. Off to the south, riders can see the Silver Creek and Middle Fork Payette River drainages; to the north, the granite-studded peaks mark the headwaters of the Salmon River's south fork. To the east is the Peace Rock wilderness study area. The ride back to the vehicle is a screamer; watch out for tight corners.

Interpretive remarks: The Silver Creek area, including the lookout, is part of an experimental forest. Researchers for the Boise National Forest are studying the effect of various logging methods and erosion-control techniques, including paved roads, on water quality and sediment runoff. The area's white granitic soils are highly erosive; the area is part of the Idaho Batholith geologic formation.

Possible sidetrip: Turn left at the logging spur on the way to the lookout (seven-tenths of a mile) and explore an old clearcut. Don't get lost -- the road forks numerous times and it's not maintained.

Other activities: Camping, fishing, hot springs soaking (Boiling Springs and Silver Creek Plunge are only a few miles away) and hiking.

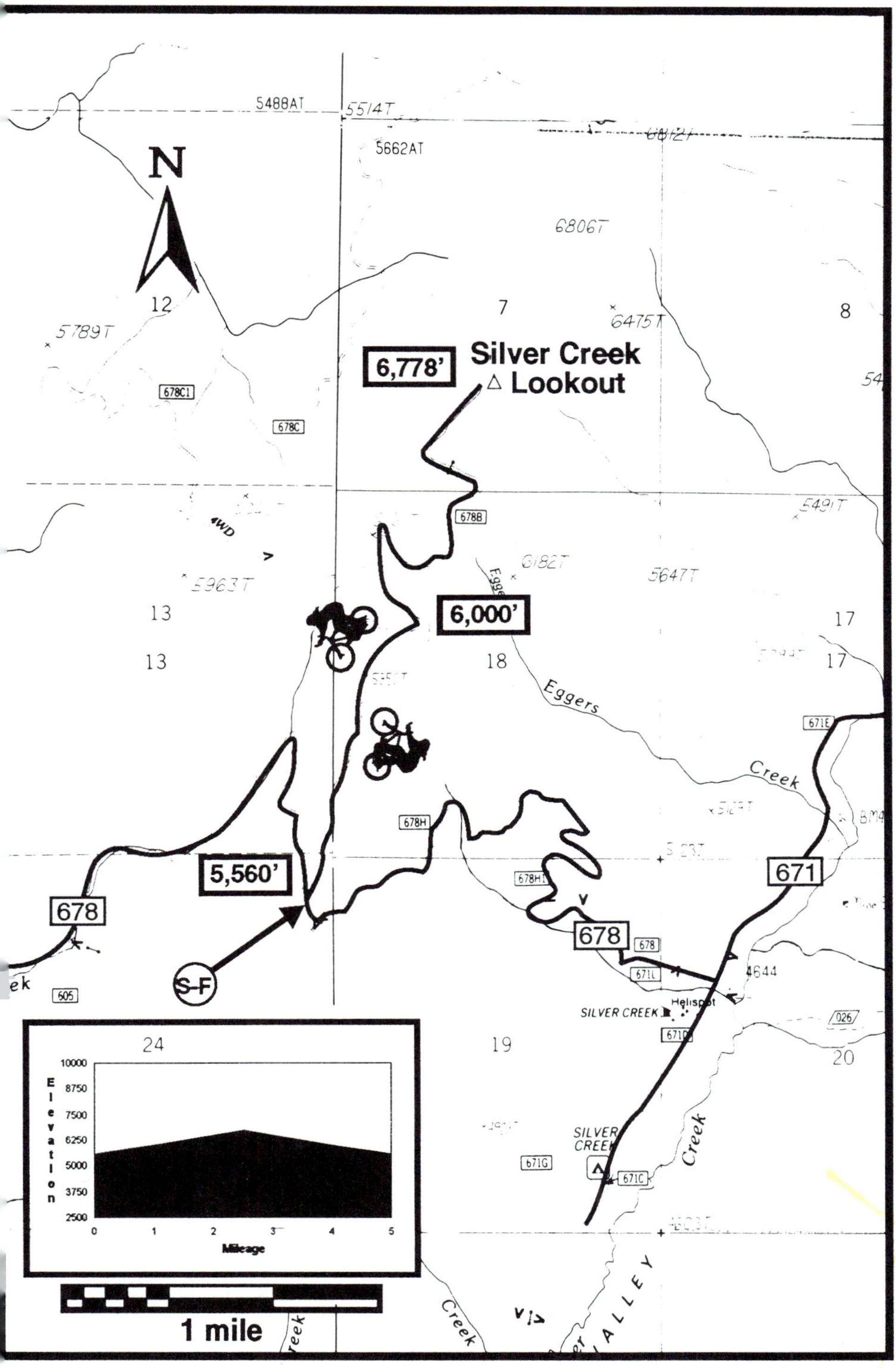
N
5488AT
5514T
5662AT
6806T
12
7
8
5789T
6475T
6,778'
Silver Creek
Lookout
678C1
678C
678B
4WD
6182T
5647T
5963T
13
13
6,000'
17
17
18
Eggers
Creek
671E
678H
5,560'
671
678
678HI
678
678
671L
4644
S-F
605
Helispot
SILVER CREEK
026
671D
24
19
20
10000
8750
7500
6250
5000
3750
2500
Elevation
0
1
2
3
4
5
Mileage
SILVER
CREEK
671G
671C
Creek
1 mile
Creek
VALLEY

INTERMEDIATE RIDES

PILOT PEAK LOOKOUT

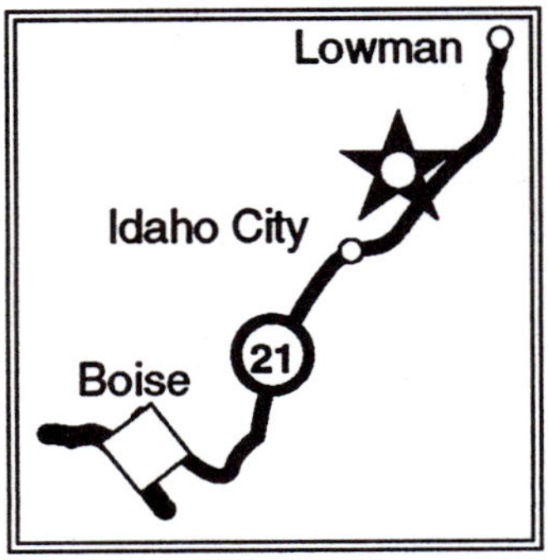

Quality: ***
Distance: 8.5 miles (4.25 miles one-way)
Difficulty: Intermediate
Riding time: 1.5-3 hours
Trail: 4WD dirt road
Season: June-October
Caution: Rough road; the downhill will rattle your teeth.
Watch out for: Motorcycles and 4WD vehicles
Topo: Sunset Mountain

Getting there: From Boise, drive east on Idaho 21 past Idaho City for 13 miles to Mores Creek Summit. Park in the large lot on the right-hand side of the pass.

The Ride: This ride features a steep hillclimb for the first couple miles, but it's worth the toil. Once on top, cyclists will enjoy a grand view of the Boise River headwaters and the Sawtooth Mountains. Stretch a little before you start: the pitch is fairly steep and continuous for the first 2 miles. To begin, cross Idaho 21 and ride up the jeep trail heading for Pilot Peak. By the 3rd mile, the road flattens a little as it nears a saddle junction at 3.25 miles. Take an immediate right to head up to the Lookout. It's about 8/10s of a mile. Enjoy the view. Return as you came.

Variations: When returning from the lookout, ride to the saddle junction, turn right and ride to the junction of Bear Run Road and USFS Road #380. Turn left toward Idaho City and ride about a half-mile to a fork. Turn right and ride a few hundred yards to an old log cabin. Explore the cabin, eat lunch and return as you came.

-- **Ride to Freeman Peak.** Turn left at the saddle junction and ride across the face of Freeman. You can ride other roads to explore the upper part of the mountain or put down your bike and hike.

-- **Return to the lot and bag Sunset Mountain.** Two peaks, two lookouts in one day! See page 12 for ride description and map.

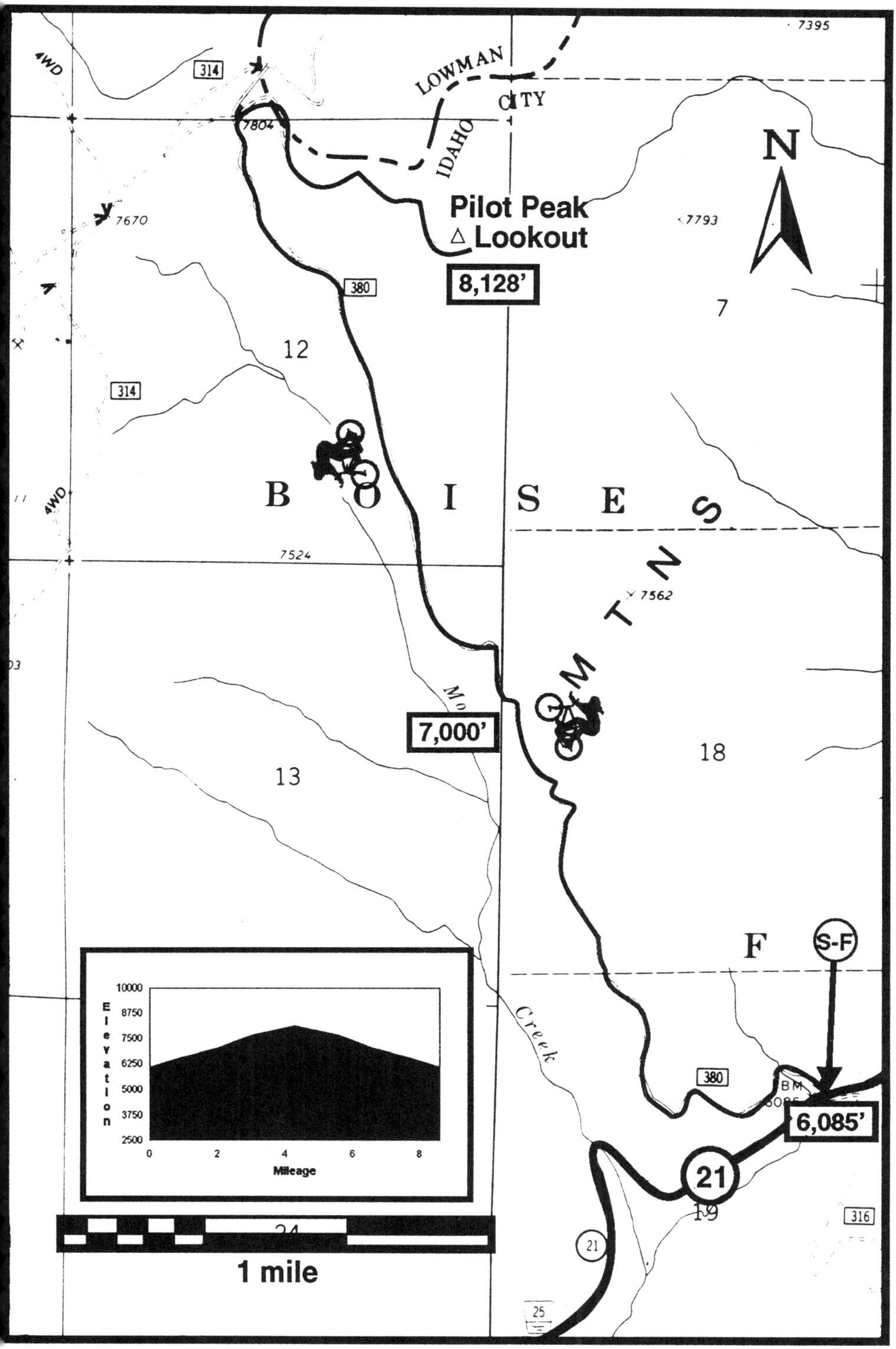

Pilot Peak
△ Lookout
8,128'
7,000'
6,085'
LOWMAN
IDAHO
CITY
BOISE
MTNS
F
S-F
N
Creek
380
314
316
21
25
7804
7670
7793
7395
7524
7562
4WD
12
13
18
7
19
24
Elevation
Mileage
1 mile

SUNSET LOOKOUT

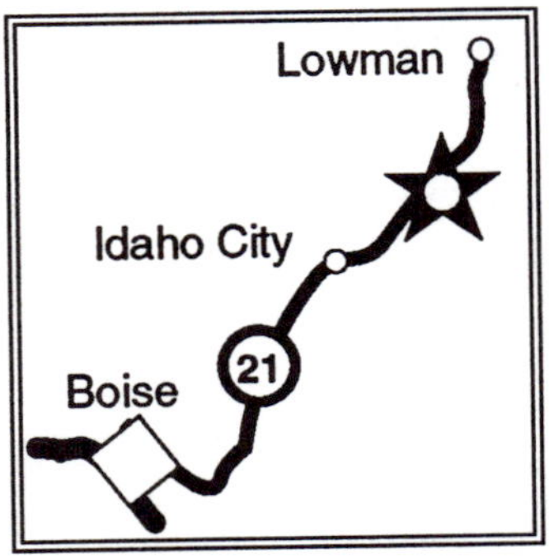

Quality: ***
Distance: 9.4 miles (4.7 one-way)
Difficulty: Intermediate
Riding time: 1.5-3 hours
Trail: 4WD road
Season: May-October
Topo map: Sunset Mountain

Getting there: From Boise, drive east on Idaho 21 past Idaho City for 13 miles to Mores Creek Summit. Park in the large lot on the right-hand side of the pass.

The Ride: This ride features a steep hillclimb for the first couple miles, but it's worth the toil. Once on top, cyclists will enjoy a grand view of the Boise River headwaters and the Sawtooth Mountains. Stretch a little before you start: the pitch is quite steep right out of the parking lot. Begin the ride by heading up the 4WD jeep trail out of the parking lot to Sunset Mountain Lookout. There's a sign at the trailhead. The first half-mile rises at a 20 percent in-your-face grade, but it eases up at about 6/10ths to a more reasonable pitch. At 7/10ths, ignore the spur peeling off to the right and stay left on the main road. At 1.2 miles, you've climbed to a point where you can see the lookout atop Sunset; there's a short downhill ahead -- let 'er rip and catch as much speed as you can because there's more climbing ahead. Two more junctions appear on the right, stay left on the main road. At 2.4 miles, the road rises at a steep gnarly pitch again for about a half-mile. Afterward, the road reaches a small saddle. Stop and take a breather and soak up the view. It's about 1.6 miles of steady uphill to the top. Sunset Mountain (elevation 7,869 feet) offers a 360-degree splendid view of the Boise River mountains, the North Fork of the Boise River, Pilot Peak (to the north), and Banner Ridge. Ask the Forest Service lookout for assistance in identifying landmarks. Return as you came.

Variations: We had hoped to chart a long downhill ride from Sunset down Hungarian Ridge to the North Fork (all single track!), but the trail has fallen into disrepair. The Boise National Forest hopes to improve the trail as soon as possible. A second trail peels off from the Lookout to the Rabbit Creek road. It's much shorter, but cyclists could follow Rabbit Creek road to the North Fork or to Idaho City, and have someone pick you up. Another variation is to ride to Sunset and Pilot Peak lookouts in one day. See Pilot Peak ride description on the previous page.

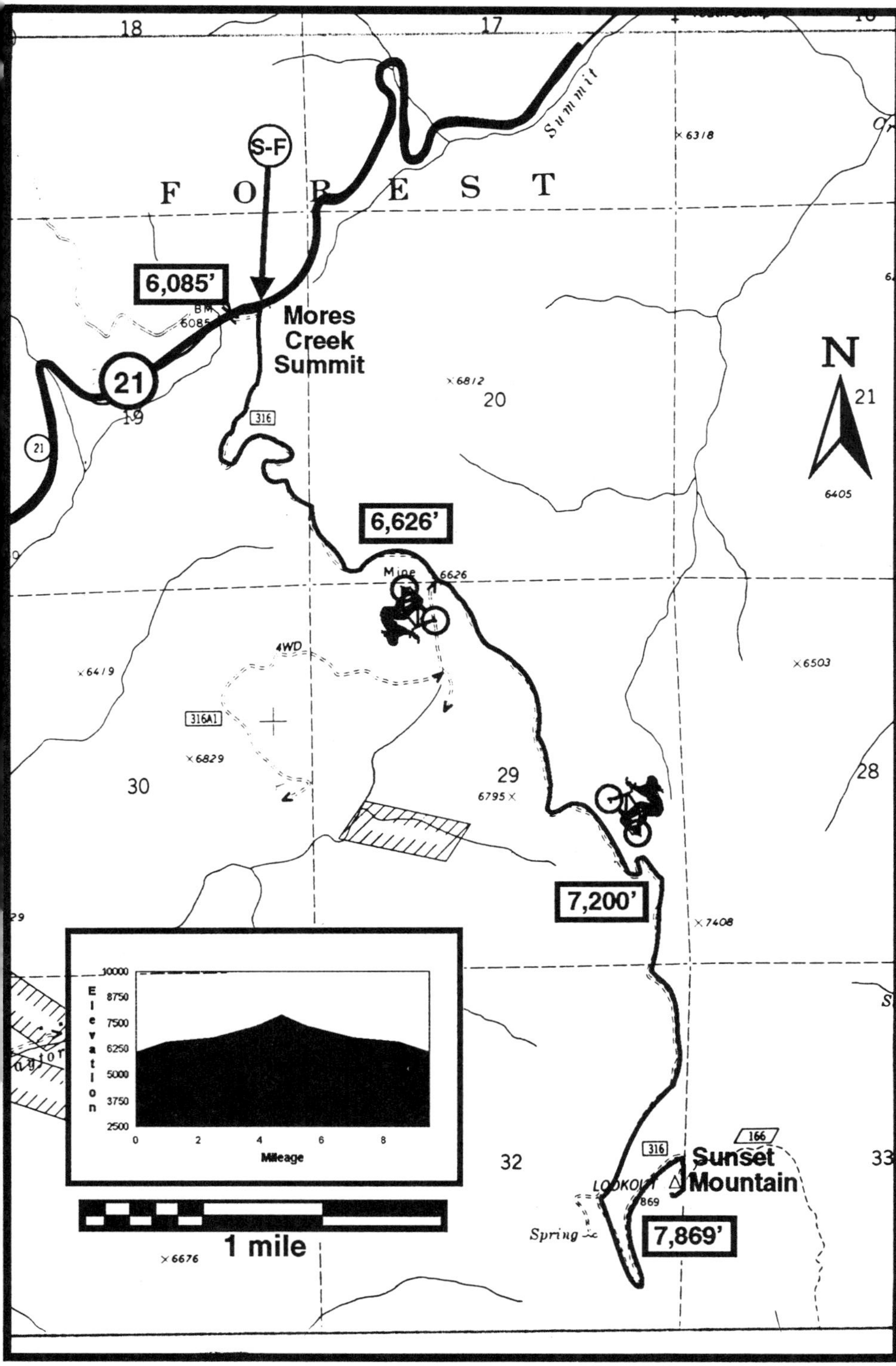
18
17
FOREST
Summit
S-F
6,085'
BM 6085
Mores Creek Summit
21
19
316
20
N
21
6405
6,626'
Mine
6626
4WD
316A1
6503
30
29
28
7,200'
7408
Elevation
Mileage
1 mile
32
33
316
166
Sunset Mountain
LOOKOUT
Spring
7,869'

PILOT PEAK/BEAR RUN ROAD

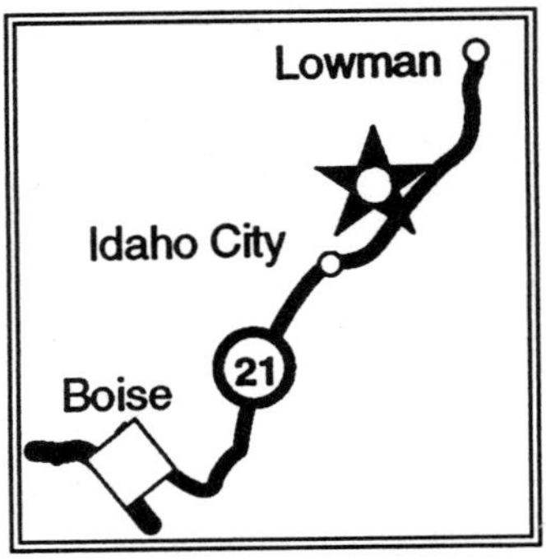

Quality: ***
Distance: 20.8 miles
Difficulty: Intermediate
Riding time: 3-3.5 hours
Trail: 4WD dirt road
Season: Late May to mid-October
Cautions: Watch out for deep ruts and vehicles on 4WD road during the screaming downhill to Idaho City.

Getting there: From Boise, take Idaho 21 to Idaho City. Drop a vehicle in the visitor's center parking lot. **(This ride requires a shuttle or hitch-hike back to Mores Creek Summit afterward).** Proceed to Mores Creek Summit and park in the big lot on the right-hand side.

The Ride: It's a short steep climb to the Pilot Peak saddle, but from there, the Bear Run ride involves an exciting, 14-mile descent into Idaho City. To begin the ride, cross the highway and climb 3.25 miles toward Pilot Peak. It's a fairly steep pitch right off the bat, so it's best to stretch out. At 3.25 miles, the road reaches a saddle and splits off three ways. Stay on the main road that curves around to the right. Just a little over a tenth of a mile later, you reach the junction with Bear Run Road (USFS Road No. 314). Watch for the sign that says "Bear Run-Idaho City." Turn left. Ride a half-mile to another junction; stay left and follow the orange snowmobile markers for Bear Run Road. At 4.14 miles, the road curves to the left, marked by an arrow on a tree. For the next 1.25 miles, the road rolls up and down until you begin the long, exhilerating descent to Idaho City. Six miles into the ride, the climbing is over. Elevation gain to this point is 1,870 feet. Cyclists will encounter numerous forks on the way down; stay on the main road by following the snowmobile markers. At about 10 miles, cyclists ride down some tight switchbacks and encounter USFS Road No. 314NA, stay on the main road. At 10.63 miles, the road forks, stay left. After riding about 14 miles, the road passes through private property and homes in Duquette Pines. Please respect residents' privacy and tread lightly. Follow Bear Run into Idaho City's main street. Turn left and pick up your vehicle.

Interpretive remarks: Bear Run Road got its name from a couple of miners, who tried to steer their competition away from rich gold deposits by saying they got chased by a bear down the area where Bear Run road is located today. Much of the forested terrain along Bear Run Road near Idaho City was mined in the 1800s for gold. Watch for trees growing out of heaps of rocks or soil left from placer mining.

Combo activities: Explore quaint Idaho City, eat lunch or stop for ice cream. Bring your camping gear, stay overnight in the national forest, and enjoy other Idaho City-area rides in the our book.

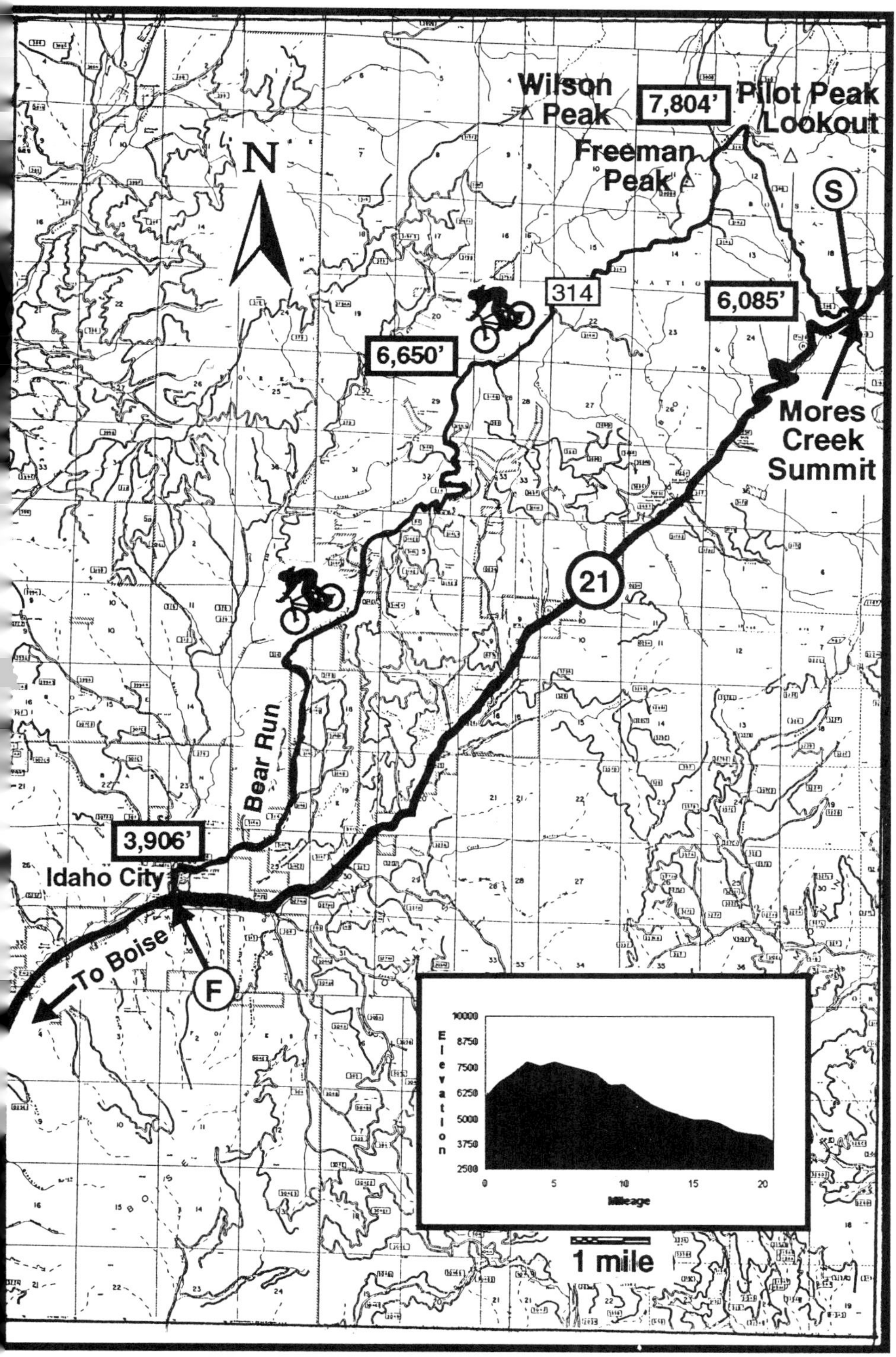
Wilson Peak
7,804'
Pilot Peak Lookout
Freeman Peak
N
S
314
6,085'
6,650'
Mores Creek Summit
21
Bear Run
3,906'
Idaho City
To Boise
F
Elevation
Mileage
10000
8750
7500
6250
5000
3750
2500
0
5
10
15
20
1 mile

BOISE BASIN INTERMEDIATE LOOP

Quality: ***
Distance: 11.2 miles
Difficulty: Intermediate
Riding time: 1.5-2.5 hours
Trail: Single-track, 2WD dirt road
Season: May-October
Watch out for: Vehicles on the road
Topo map: Shafer Butte

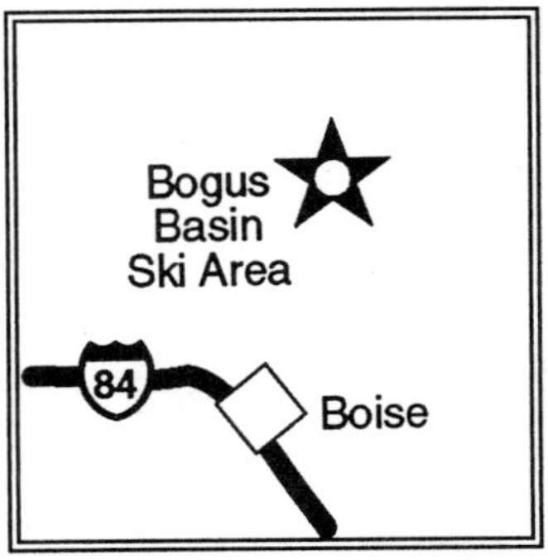

Getting there: From Boise, drive north on Bogus Basin Road about 16 miles to the ski area. Park in the large lot next to lower lodge.

The Ride: This route features some moderate climbing, enjoyable single-track riding and quick descents near Bogus Basin and Mores Mountain. Cyclists who complete this ride non-stop will receive a good workout, but you still should have some energy left for other activities in the area. Start by riding to the northwest out of the parking lot on the Boise Ridge road. Proceed past the cross-country ski hut and a metal gate (don't turn right and head for Pioneer Lodge) and continue on the dirt road. At 3.35 miles, cyclists arrive at the junction of the ridge road and Shafer Butte picnic area. Stay on the ridge road for another 1.6 miles. At mile 5, watch for a single-track trail passing on the right side of two wooden posts, which may or may not have a sign attached. Turn right and follow the trail through brush and trees for 1.6 miles. The view from the trail looks out over the old Boise Basin Mining District -- Placerville and Centerville. Tall granite rock spires rise from the mountain, revealing portions of the Idaho Batholith granitic geological formation. Leave the single-track trail at 6.6 miles and turn left on a dirt road leading to the Mores Mountain Trail (paved and lined with timbers). You have arrived at the Shafer Butte Picnic Area. From here, turn right and descend 1.2 miles to the Boise Ridge Road. Turn left and ride 3.3 miles back to your vehicle.

Interpretive remarks: In June and July, wildflowers create a rainbow of colors on the landscape. In the fall, cyclists will enjoy the bright variety of colors on shrubs and trees -- brilliant reds, yellows and greens across the mountains. Riders will notice impressive granite rocks rising from the earth on Mores Mountain. These are typical features of the Idaho Batholith, a massive granitic geological formation that extends from the Boise Front to points north of the Salmon River.

Combo activities: Plant and wildflower identification, camping, lunch at the picnic area, rock climbing on the granite spires.

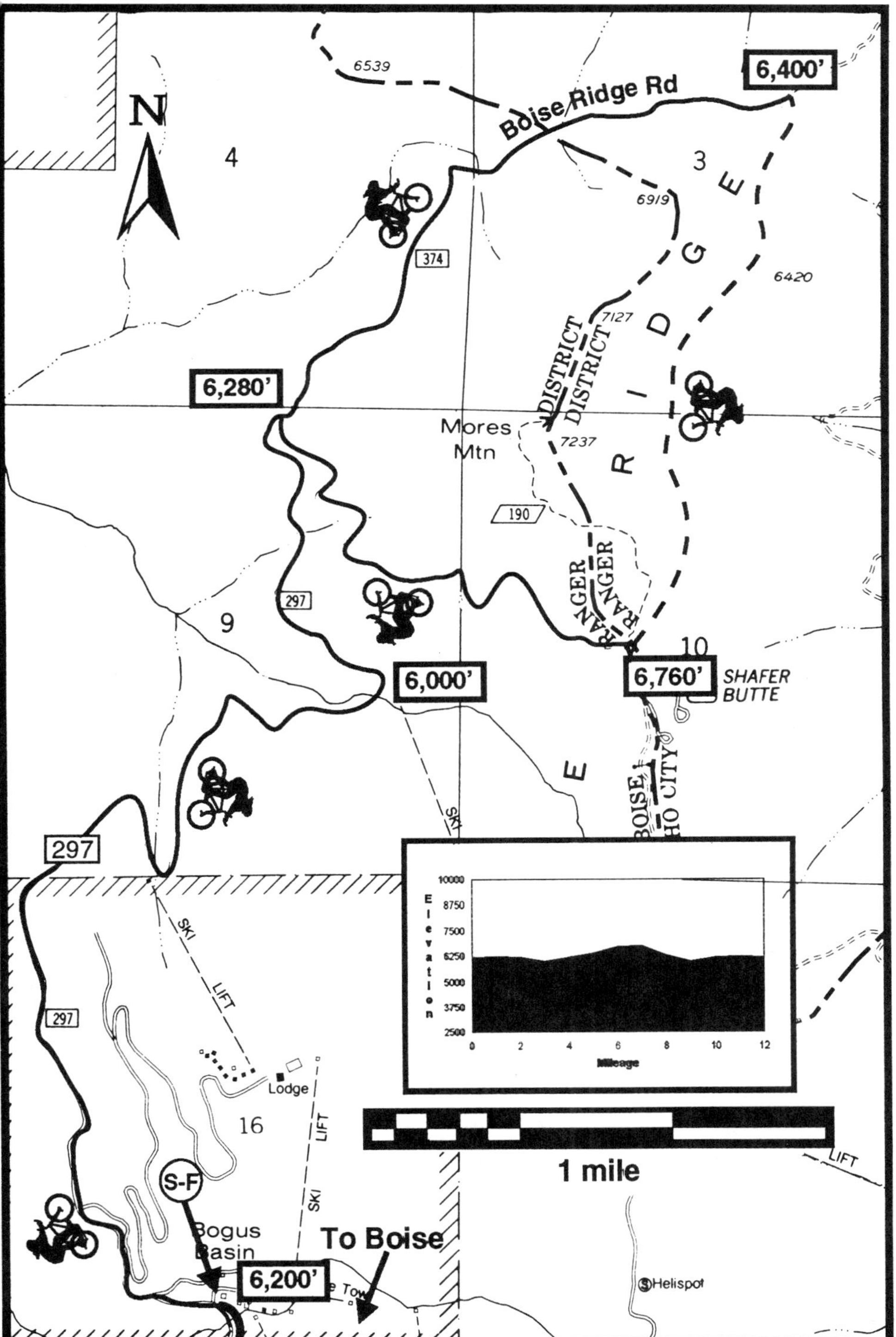
N
Boise Ridge Rd
6539
6,400'
4
3
6919
374
6420
7127
DISTRICT
RIDGE
6,280'
Mores
Mtn
7237
190
RANGER
297
9
10
6,000'
6,760'
SHAFER
BUTTE
BOISE
SKI
297
Elevation
10000
8750
7500
6250
5000
3750
2500
0
2
4
6
8
10
12
Mileage
SKI
LIFT
297
Lodge
16
LIFT
SKI
1 mile
S-F
Bogus
Basin
To Boise
6,200'
LIFT
Helispot

TOUR DE BOGUS BASIN

Quality: ****
Distance: 13.25 miles
Difficulty: Intermediate
Riding time: 2-3 hours
Trail: 4WD dirt road, single-track
Season: May-October
Cautions: Yield to other trail users
Topo maps: Shafer Butte, Robie Creek

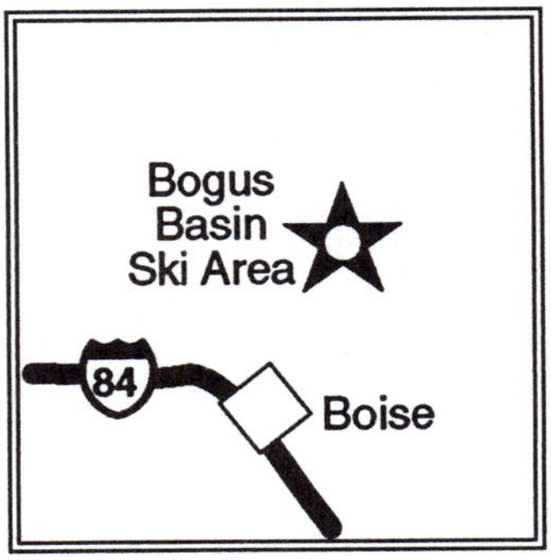

Getting there: Drive up Bogus Basin Road 13.3 miles from Highlands Elementary School and watch for a 2WD dirt road leading off to the right. Park in the dirt lot on the right. The area is marked as a no-parking zone, but it is enforced only in the winter.

The Ride: This is an excellent escape-the-heat ride and outstanding global tour of the ski area in the summer. Pedal up the 2WD dirt road that heads for Deer Point. At the top of the first little hill, stay left. Proceed for 2.11 miles to a junction with Doe Point and the Boise Ridge roads, go left, hop over the gate, and continue toward Doe Point. Stay on the road away from the radio towers and ride under Chair #1 (Deer Point) on the road heading northeast to the Showcase chairlift. Ride toward the Pine Creek cutoff; at mile 2.74, turn right. Follow the 4WD road to the intersection with Nugget. Watch for a left-hand turn indicating "easiest way down" at mile 3.86. The sandy road descends on a steep pitch toward the bottom of Chair #6 (Pine Creek). Follow the road behind the chairlift and catch the faint single-track heading uphill at the base of the lift. Ignore the right-hand forks. The road gets steeper as it turns up a ski run at 5.1 miles. Ride another quarter mile and exit off the ski run onto a road marked by a towering ponderosa pine tree. The road meets another ski slope; turn left and push your bike up the slope about 200 yards to the bottom of Paradise. Here, at 5.9 miles, turn left onto a main 4WD road crossing the slope and head for Majestic. After climbing a mile, you reach a saddle junction splitting three ways at 6.95 miles. Turn left and head toward the top of Shafer Butte, following several switchbacks. After the 4th switchback, you have the option of riding to the top for a big view or following the 4WD road toward the Pioneer Lodge. Pass under Chair #3 (Superior) and ride downhill to the lodge. Pass by the tennis courts to the left and follow a road that traverses the top of the beginner slopes; eventually the road exits to the paved road leading to Pioneer Lodge. Go left and return to your vehicle.

Variations: Many variations are possible in this ride. Two options arise at the 6.95-mile saddle junction. From here, you could turn right and ride to the bottom of Chair #3, then to the Boise Ridge Road and back to the vehicle. Or, you could turn right and head for the Shafer Butte Picnic Area, and then circle back on the ridge road to your vehicle. At the Pioneer Lodge, there are several other roads leading to the lower lodge instead of taking the paved road down. Be sure to study the topo map before attempting variations.

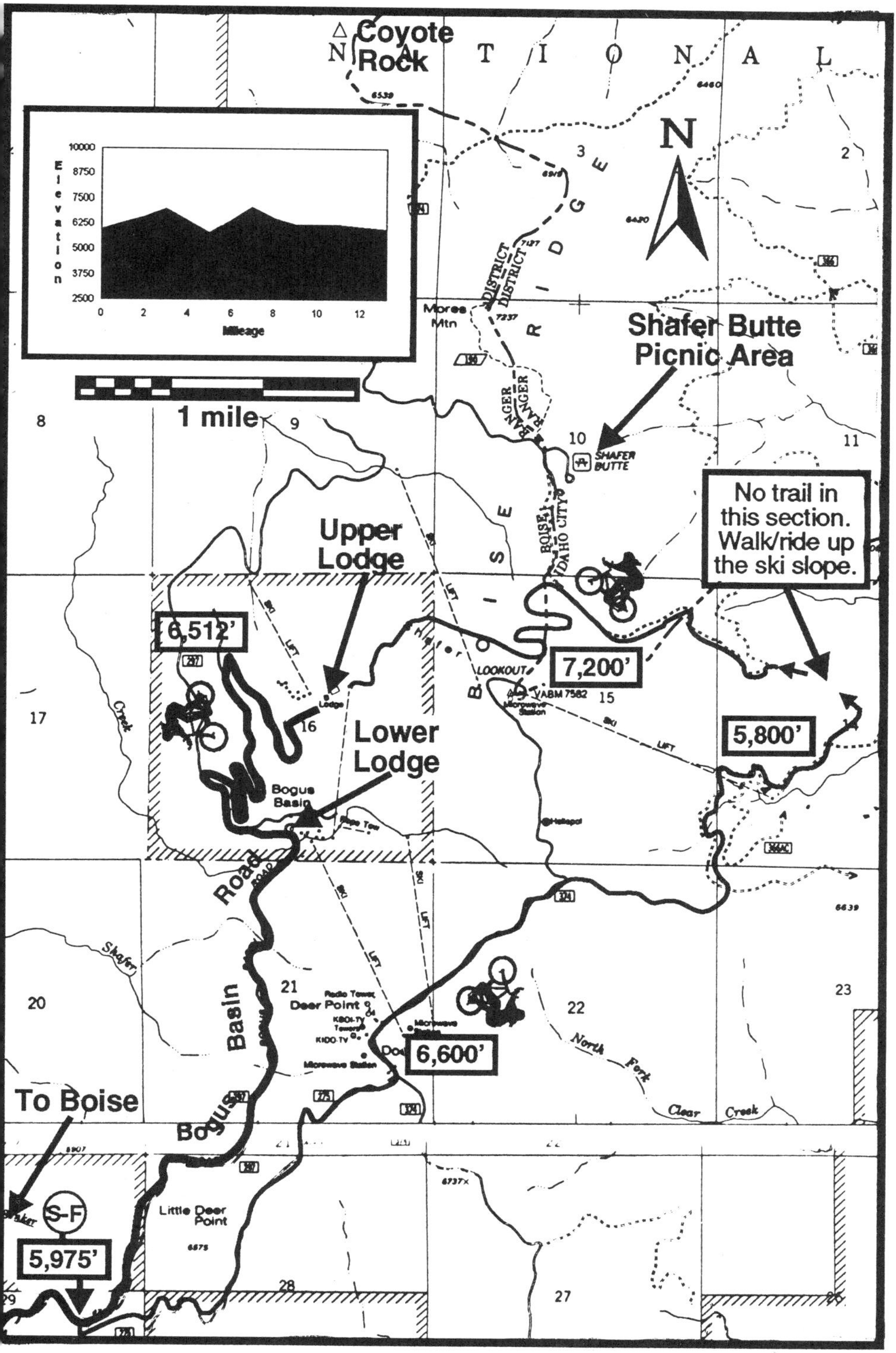

Coyote Rock
N A T I O N A L
B O I S E R I D G E
N
Elevation
Mileage
1 mile
Mores Mtn
Shafer Butte Picnic Area
Upper Lodge
Lower Lodge
No trail in this section. Walk/ride up the ski slope.
6,512'
7,200'
5,800'
6,600'
5,975'
LOOKOUT
Bogus Basin
Deer Point
Little Deer Point
North Fork
Clear Creek
To Boise
Bogus Basin Road
S-F

IDAHO CITY-CHARCOAL GULCH

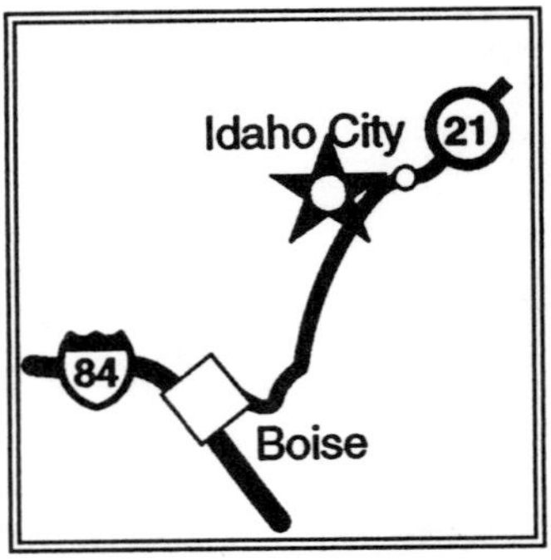

Quality: ****
Distance: 6 miles
Difficulty: Advanced beginner
Riding time: 1-2 hours
Trail: 2WD road, 4WD road, single-track trail
Season: May-October
Cautions: Watch out for traffic in Slaughterhouse Gulch (USFS Road #307).
Topo map: Idaho City

Getting there: From Boise, take Idaho 21 about 45 miles to Idaho City. Park in the Visitor's Center lot, the school lot, or somewhere in town.

The Ride: This ride is an easy-going loop that involves climbing 1,000 vertical feet over 3.5 miles to Charcoal Gulch and an invigorating descent. To begin, ride to a junction just before the Idaho City school, turn left and follow signs for Centerville. The 2WD dirt road, USFS Road #307, peels out of Idaho City in the northwest corner of town and the pavement ends. The popular, washboard-prone dirt road climbs about 3.5 miles (approximate) to a summit; watch for a sign indicating "landfill," and turn left at the sign. Follow the road about 100 feet or so and watch for the trail dropping down Charcoal Gulch on the left. The trail is marked by a yellow caution sign on a pine tree. From here, it's a 1.5-mile thrilling descent on single-track trail down the gulch. Watch out for other trail users and stay on the main trail heading downhill. At mile 5, the trail comes to a T-junction with a 4WD dirt road leading back to the airport, turn left. It's a half-mile back to the airport and another half-mile back to town.

Interpretive remarks: Charcoal Gulch is a fun place to go cross-country skiing in the winter.

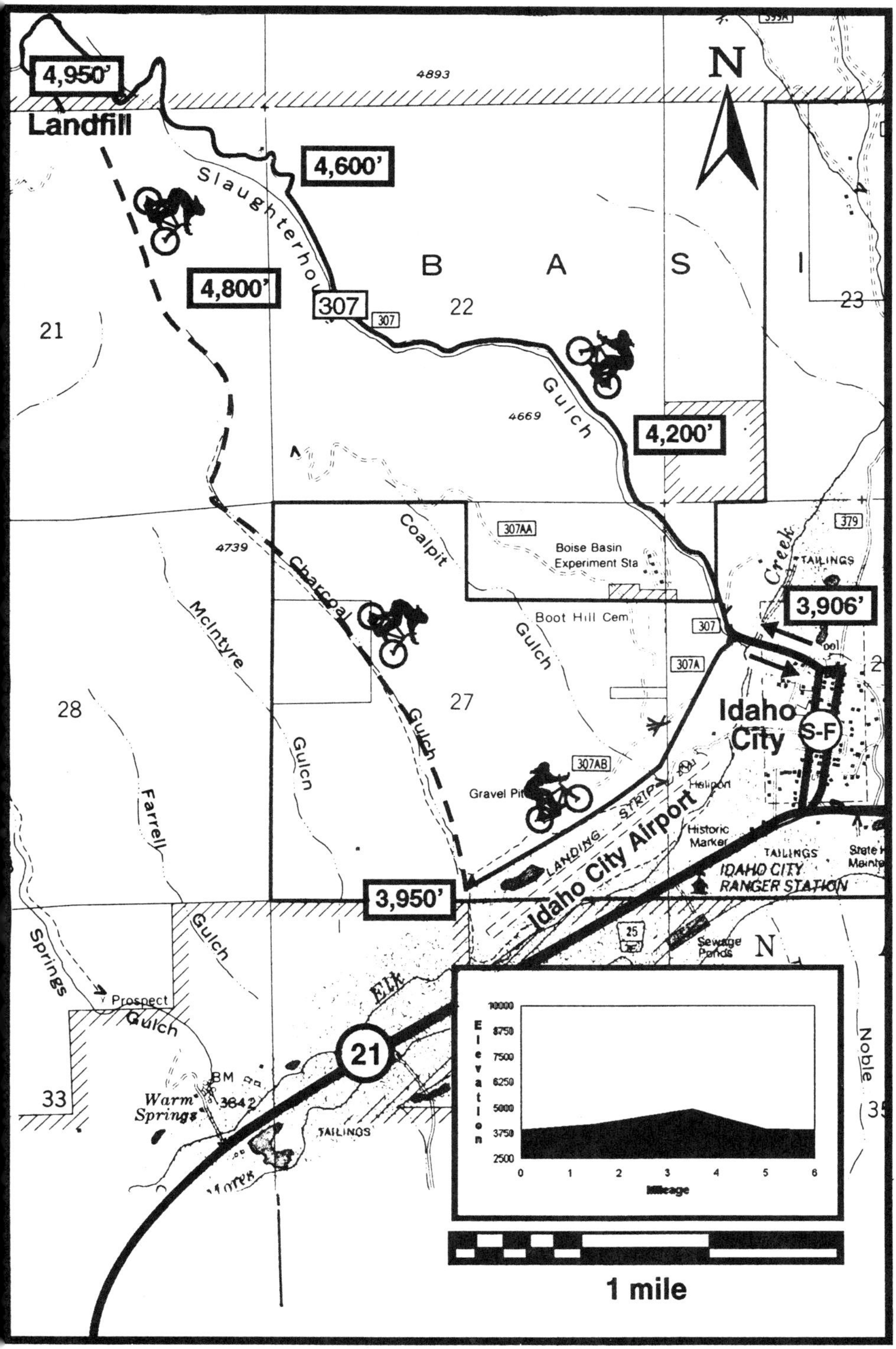
4,950'
Landfill
4893
N
4,600'
Slaughterhouse
4,800'
307
22
B A S I
23
21
Gulch
4669
4,200'
307AA
Boise Basin Experiment Sta
4739
Charcoal
Coalpit
McIntyre
Boot Hill Cem
Gulch
Creek
TAILINGS
379
3,906'
307
307A
28
27
Idaho City
S-F
Gulch
Gulch
307AB
Gravel Pit
Heliport
Farrell
Landing Strip
Idaho City Airport
Historic Marker
TAILINGS
IDAHO CITY RANGER STATION
3,950'
Gulch
25
Sewage Ponds
Springs
Prospect Gulch
Elk
21
BM 3842
Warm Springs
33
TAILINGS
Noble
Elevation
10000
8750
7500
6250
5000
3750
2500
0 1 2 3 4 5 6
Mileage
1 mile

BUNNY CREEK LOOP

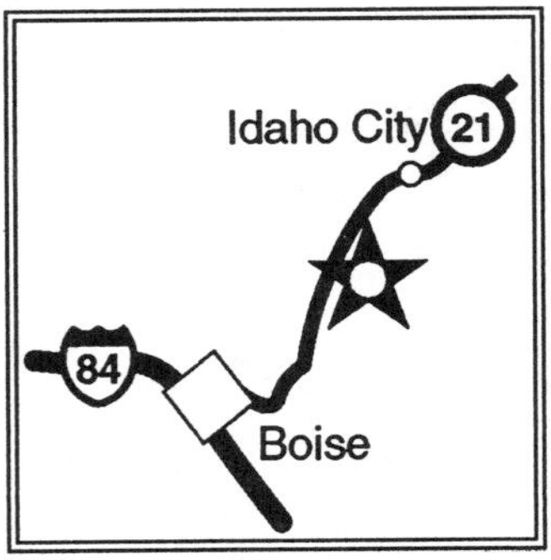

Quality: ****
Distance: 11 miles
Difficulty: advanced-intermediate
Riding time: 2-3.5 miles
Trail: Single-track, 4WD road, hike-a-bike
Season: May-October
Caution: This ride has numerous technical sections and hazards that appear quicky. Ride carefully.

Getting there: From Boise, drive east on Idaho 21 toward Idaho City about 31 miles to the Thorn Creek lookout/Cottonwood Creek Road junction. Turn right and drive seven miles to the junction of USFS Roads Nos. 377, 202 and 203. Park here.

The Ride: Ride about 4.8 miles up the Thorn Creek Lookout Road (USFS Road #203) to the Bunny Creek trailhead on the left-hand side. The trailhead is marked only by a small cairn, the remains of a dispersed campground, a meadow on the right, and a group of six pine trees. Pay attention, it is difficult to find the trail. The trail starts about 50 feet off to the left side of the road in the group of six pine trees. The first 100 yards of the trail involve a steep, technical descent; we strongly recommend you walk the first time you try it. At the bottom of the first hill, ride through a short section of thick vegetation and trees along the ridge. At 5.5 miles, the trail comes into a clearing and, almost immediately, you will be forced off the bike and walk up a steep, barren sidehill. Reach the summit at 5.63 miles and fight off a little more thick brush. Hang in there because at 5.89 miles, you start descending along an open ridge. It's time to stop and enjoy the gorgeous vistas surrounding you. The descent continues for another mile until the trail bends left at the 7-mile mark and you drop off the east side of the ridge. Follow the trail around a hill on your right to a large open area. This can be a grassy meadow or a barren parcel of dirt depending on the amount of recent rainfall and deer/elk grazing that's occurred (7.7 miles).
Descend off the left (east) side of this opening and you arrive at Bunny Creek for the first time. Turn west at the creek (downhill) and ride along the left bank. Again, it's rough-going along the creek, but don't get discouraged -- the trail soon becomes a smooth winding single track. The downhill along Bunny Creek is a hoot, but keep your speed down -- the trail deteriorates to sand or powdery dust. At 9 miles, you'll intersect the main Forest Service road #377. Turn left and pedal uphill about 2.1 miles to your car.

Interpretive remarks: Wildflowers abound along the Easter Creek ride. Among the flowers you will see in July-August are: scarlet gilia (bright red trumpet-shaped flowers), yarrow (white or yellow tiny flowers clustered together), pink geraniums, and sulfur flowers (yellow -- sometimes called the umbrella plant). If you crush the yarrow leaves, they will produce a very distinctive odor. They have been used to make tea. Watch for wildlife on this ride, particularly deer and elk.

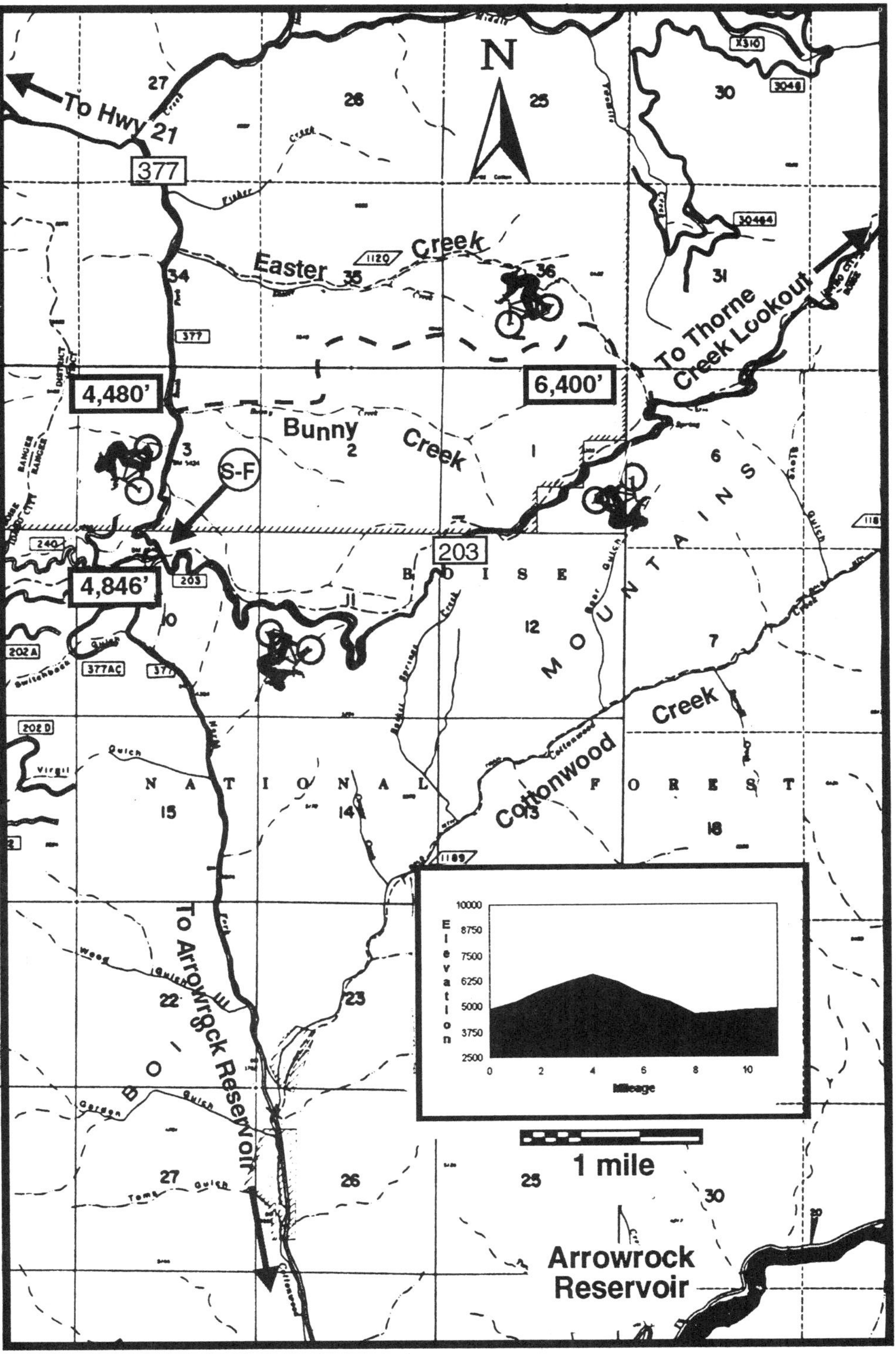

To Hwy 21
377
N
Easter Creek
1120
To Thorne Creek Lookout
4,480'
6,400'
Bunny Creek
S-F
203
4,846'
BOISE MOUNTAINS
NATIONAL FOREST
Cottonwood Creek
To Arrowrock Reservoir
Elevation
Mileage
1 mile
Arrowrock Reservoir

BOISE RIDGE LOOP

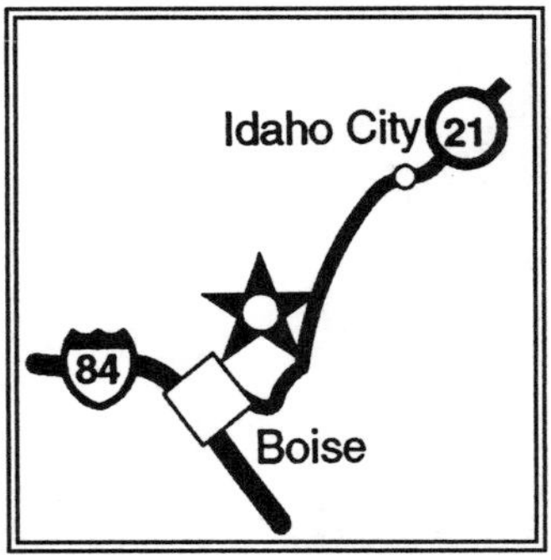

Quality: **
Distance: 23 miles
Difficulty: Advanced intermediate
Riding time: 2.75-4 hours
Trail: 4WD dirt road, 2WD dirt road
Season: May-October
Watch out for: Motorcycles and vehicles
Topo maps: Boise North, Robie Creek

Getting there: From Boise, drive north on Eighth Street until it turns into a dirt road. The ride starts here.

The Ride: The Boise Ridge Loop features a long, challenging climb involving 3,000 feet of vertical gain up Eighth Street and then a long descent down the ridge and Rocky Canyon Road back to Boise. This is an excellent route for building endurance. Start slow and spin easy gears to save energy. Proceed up Eighth Street for about 8 miles to the Boise Ridge Road, turn right. Take a minute to soak up the views and recover from the arduous climb. However, there's still a few switchbacks to the top of the ridge. Follow the ridge road toward Aldape Summit -- it's about 5.25 miles. Turn right on Rocky Canyon and plunge downhill to Shaw Mountain Road. Take it slow in the washboard-ridden sections of the dirt road -- the bumps shake your arms and body to the point where your teeth may fall out. It's six miles of downhill to the paved road at the bottom. Follow the road to the junction of Table Rock Road and Shaw Mountain Road. Turn right and head back to Boise. Shaw Mountain turns into Reserve Street as it winds past Fort Boise. To reach Eighth Street, follow Reserve to the first stop sign at Fort Street. Turn right and proceed to Eighth Street. Turn right and head back to your vehicle.

Variations: Reverse the loop by climbing Rocky Canyon Road to the Boise Ridge Road, climb the ridge to Eighth Street, and descend down Eighth Street back to Boise. The climb is steeper in this direction.

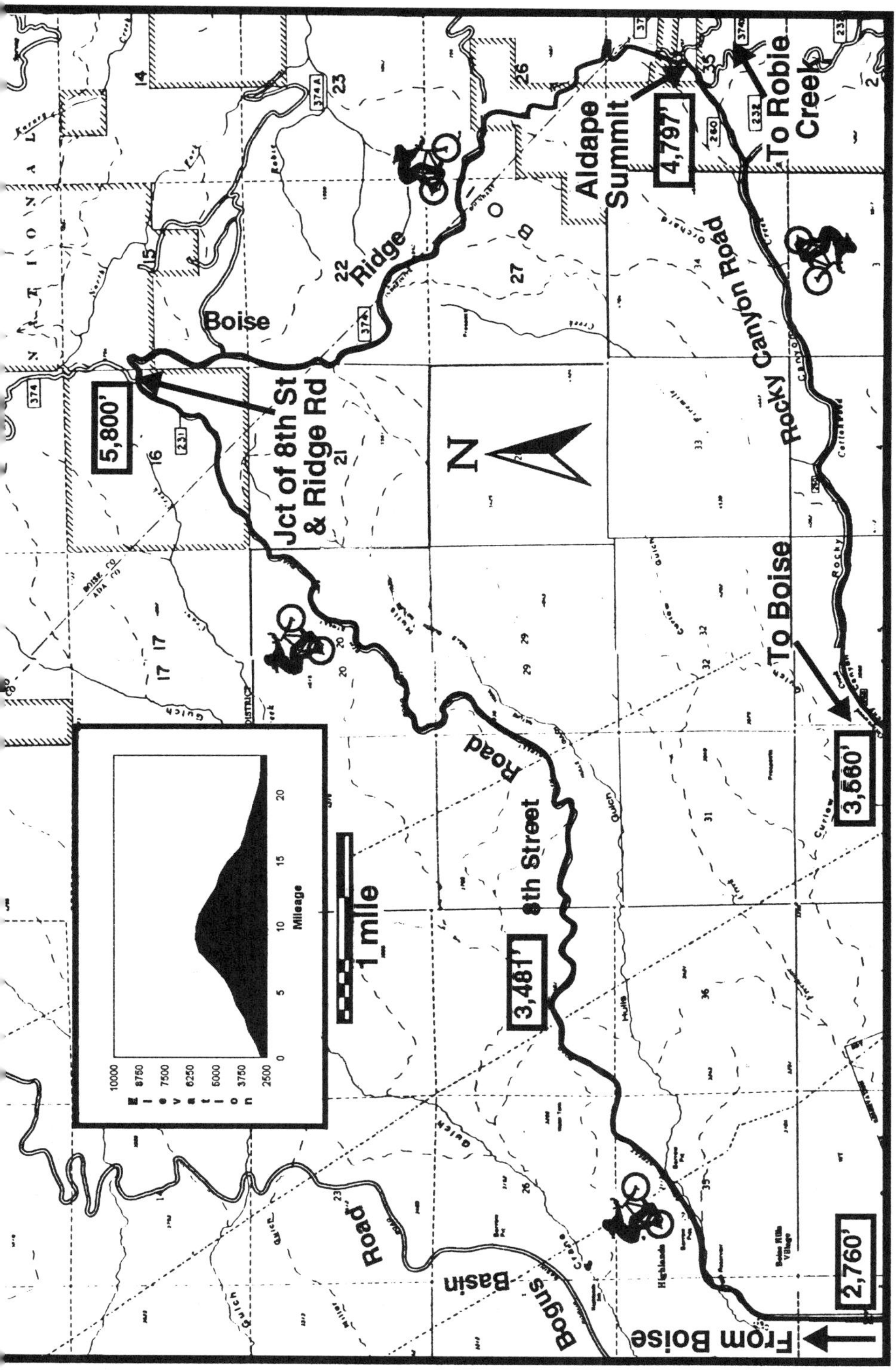
From Boise
2,760'
Bogus Basin Road
3,481'
8th Street Road
1 mile
Elevation
10000
8750
7500
6250
5000
3750
2500
0
5
10
15
20
Mileage
5,800'
Jct of 8th St & Ridge Rd
Boise Ridge
N
Aldape Summit
4,797'
To Robie Creek
Rocky Canyon Road
To Boise
3,560'

SILVER CREEK SUMMIT

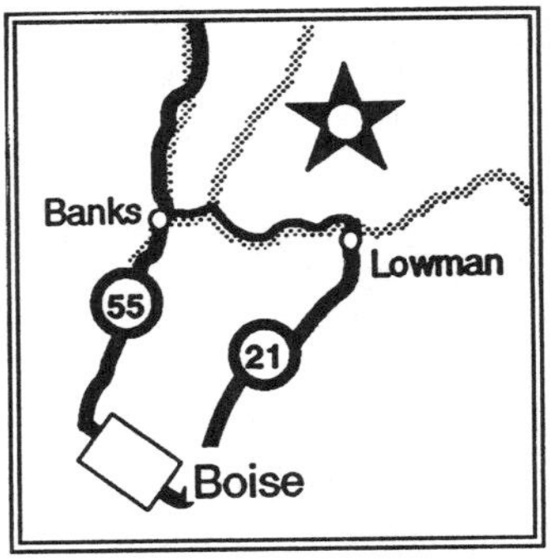

Quality: ****
Distance: 3.5 miles; 7 miles roundtrip
Difficulty: Intermediate
Riding time: 45-90 minutes to the summit
Trail: Single-track trail
Season: late May-October
Watch out for: ATVs, motorcycles

Getting there: From Boise, drive north on Idaho 55 about 34 miles to Banks. Cross the bridge, turn right and drive about eight miles to the Crouch turnoff; turn left. Go 24 miles north to the junction with USFS Road #678 (just before Boiling Springs Campground), turn right. Proceed 7 miles to the junction with Silver Creek (stay right when you reach the intersection of (USFS #678B). Turn left. Follow the road to a deadend; the trail up to Silver Creek summit is on the left; the ride starts here.

The Ride: For the first mile or so, the wide, sandy trail follows the headwaters of Silver Creek; it is shaded by tall Engleman spruce and Douglas fir trees. The grade increases as cyclists near the top. Riders will enjoy the trail's ideal width -- it's not real narrow, and it's not real wide. For the entire 3.5 miles, the scenery is outstanding, particularly in the fall -- big granite slabs, red alder brush, a variety of wildflowers, yellow and red aspen leaves, and expansive views. The ride climbs from about 4,800 feet to 6,250 feet at the summit, a vertical rise of 1,450 feet or 415 per mile. The final half-mile is the steepest part of the trail; our advice is to grunt it out and try to stay on your bike. The views from the top are outstanding, particularly of the large granite rocks and the fall colors. If you've got any energy left, stash your bikes and walk either ridgeline to the peaks for the best views.

Interpretive remarks: Keep your eyes peeled for wildlife.

Possible sidetrips: Stay on the trail and drop into Bull Creek or ride to Stolle Meadows along the South Fork of the Salmon River via the Monument Trail. If you do, however, it's a monster shuttle back to the Silver Creek area (unless someone dropped you off). Or, drop into Bull Creek and visit the hot springs along Bull Creek and the Middle Fork of the Payette River. The ride back could be grueling unless you get someone to meet you at Boiling Springs.

Other activities: Camping, fishing, hot springs soaking (Boiling Springs and Silver Creek Plunge are only a few miles away) and hiking.

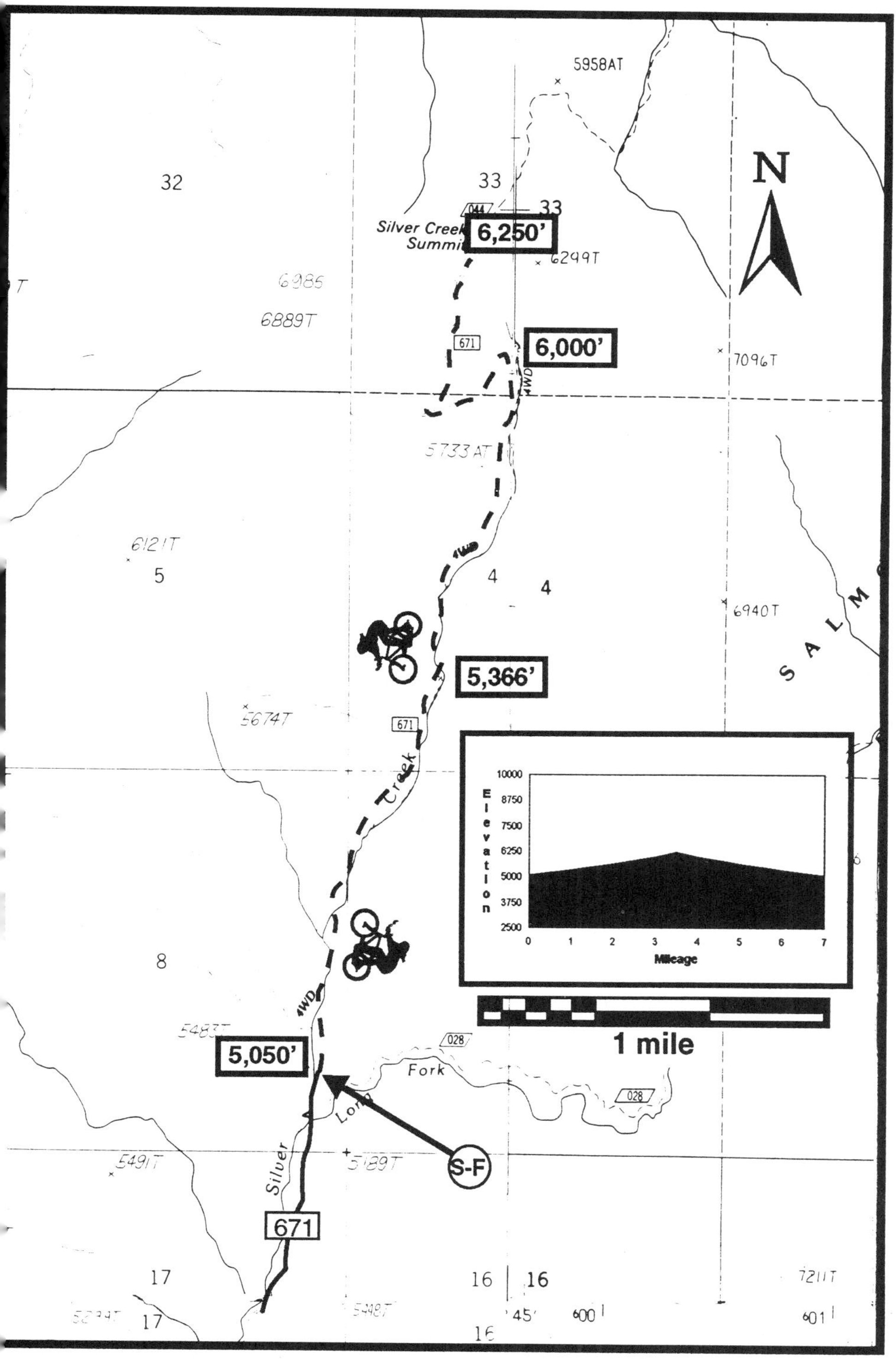
5958AT
N
32
33
33
044
Silver Creek Summit
6,250'
6299T
6985
6889T
671
6,000'
7096T
4WD
5733AT
6121T
5
4
4
6940T
SALMON
5,366'
5674T
671
Creek
10000
8750
7500
6250
5000
3750
2500
Elevation
0
1
2
3
4
5
6
7
Mileage
8
4WD
028
1 mile
5,050'
Fork
028
Long
Silver
5491T
5189T
S-F
671
17
16
16
7211T
17
45'
600
601
16

BRUNEAU FOOTHILLS LOOP

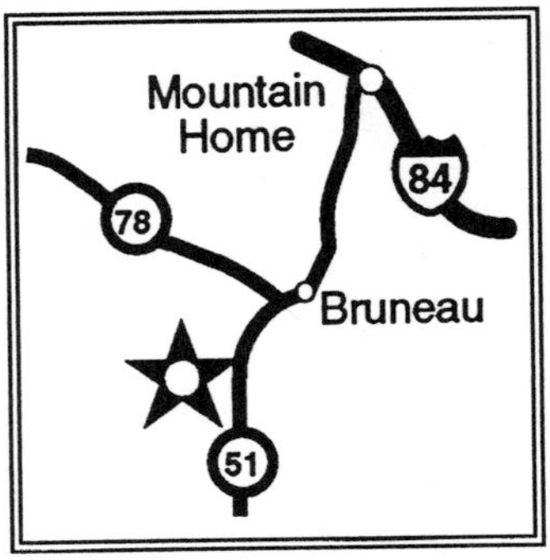

Quality: ***
Distance: 15 miles
Difficulty: Intermediate
Riding time: 1.5-4 hours
Season: Year-round depending on weather
Trail: 2WD, 4WD, short hike-a-bike in deep sand

Getting there: From Boise, take I-84 east to Mountain Home, take the first exit into town, and turn right on Idaho 51 heading for Bruneau. Proceed two miles past Bruneau on Idaho 51 to the well-marked junction with Idaho 78, turn left. Eight miles later, watch for milepost 61 on the left-hand side of the road. At the milepost, turn right onto a 2WD dirt road. Follow it to a pump house and tall radio tower. Turn left onto a two-track road and follow it to the base of the foothills. Turn right and park.

The Ride: The Bruneau desert loop is a rolling, scenic ride that roams through the Jack's Creek country and desert plateau. The ride starts along a flat two-track road heading west at the base of the foothills. At 2.3 miles, turn right onto a dirt road paralleling the pipeline to the south. At 3.5 miles, turn left onto a two-track road and follow it for 2/10ths to a faint two-track road bending to the left. Turn left. At mile 4.6, the road drops off the plateau; stay right and ride two-tenths of a mile to a junction marked by a mound of packed gravel. Turn right and follow the two-track road downhill. At 5.1 miles, ignore the right-hand fork and drop into the Jack's Creek valley floor. A mile later, the road crosses the entrance to Big Jack's Creek -- a good spot to leave the bikes, eat lunch and explore the magnificent canyon. Cross the creek and follow the two-track down the valley. The road eventually climbs back to the top of the plateau at 7.9 miles. Go straight at the top of the hill, ride two-tenths of a mile farther, and turn right onto a 2WD gravel road. At 8.3 miles, turn right onto a faint two-track and enjoy a gentle downhill to a dry creek bottom. At 9.5 miles, turn left into the creek bottom and follow it for a half-mile or so. At 9.9 miles, watch for a cow trail on the left bank of the creek, it's easier going. At 10.2 miles, cross the creek to the right bank and note another vertical-walled canyon and a tunnel drilled into the right wall. Take a second to explore. To complete the ride, cross the creek again, pick up a two-track road on the left side and follow it up a draw. At 11 miles, riders come to a T-junction. Turn right and ride downhill to a cattle guard on the flats at mile 12.8. Turn right on a faint two-track that parallels the fence on the south side. At mile 13.2, go through the gate and follow a two-track road up the hill. On top, you should be able to see the radio tower where the ride started. At mile 13.6, cross a dry wash to the left and follow a single-track trail alongside the meandering, sandy wash. The trail gets sketchy for the next half-mile, but keep heading east toward the tower along the wash. You may have to walk due to deep sand. At 14.1 miles, you'll come to a two-track road, turn right toward the foothills for about 100 yards. Watch for a left-hand turn peeling off the two-track toward the radio tower and your rig. It's less than a half-mile to your vehicle.

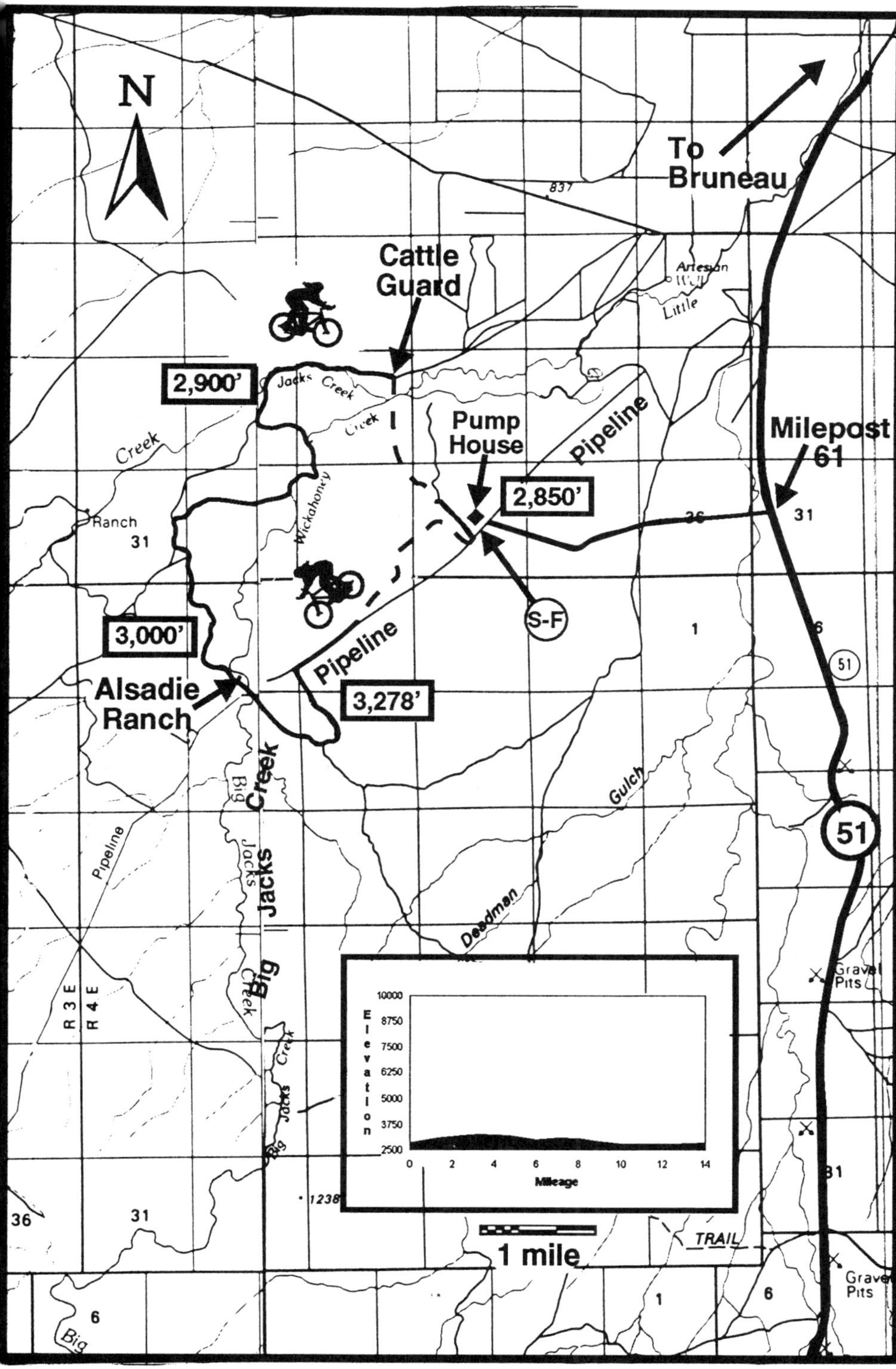
N
To Bruneau
837
Cattle Guard
Artesian Well
Little
2,900'
Jacks Creek
Creek
Creek
Pump House
Pipeline
Milepost 61
2,850'
36
31
Ranch
31
Wickahoney
S-F
1
3,000'
Pipeline
6
51
Alsadie Ranch
3,278'
Gulch
Big Creek
Big Jacks Creek
51
Pipeline
Jacks
Deadman
Gravel Pits
R 3 E
R 4 E
Big Creek
Jacks Creek
Big Jacks
Elevation
10000
8750
7500
6250
5000
3750
2500
0
2
4
6
8
10
12
14
Mileage
1238
31
36
31
TRAIL
1 mile
Gravel Pits
1
6
6
Big

AVONDALE BASIN LOOP

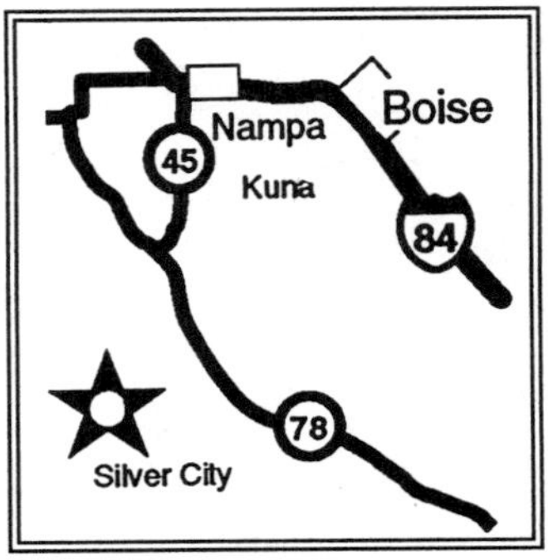

Quality: ****
Distance: 6.4 miles
Difficulty: Intermediate
Riding time: 1-2 hours
Trail: Single-track, 4WD dirt road
Season: May-October
Topo maps: Silver City; Rooster Comb Peak

Getting there: Drive to downtown Nampa and take Idaho 45 south toward Melba. Stay on Idaho 45 until you reach a junction with Idaho 78, go left toward Murphy. Proceed through Murphy and it's four miles to the Silver City turnoff on the right. The turn is marked, and it's 19 miles of bumpy, washboard-ridden dirt road to the quaint, old mining town nestled in a high basin of the Owyhee Mountains at 6,300 feet. Drive over the New York Summit to a junction marked by a permanent outhouse at 18 miles. Turn right and follow the dirt road toward DeLamar for 1.3 miles. After the main road crosses Jordan Creek, watch for an undeveloped campground along the stream. Park. The ride starts here.

The ride: From the campground, ride downstream along the bank, cross the creek, and look for a major single-track trail heading up Presby Creek toward Avondale Basin. Follow the trail as it winds up the gentle draw through sagebrush and juniper trees. At 1.5 miles, the trail begins to level out and meanders through a desert alpine meadow. At 2.7 miles, the trail confronts a small meadow marked by a broken-down corral. Go straight across the meadow to the right of the corral and pick up the trail, which forks shortly afterward. Go left (a right-hand turn takes you to New York Summit) and follow the single track toward the ridgetop. At 3.1 miles is another junction, stay left on the main trail. At 3.8 miles, the trail reaches the summit for a glorious view of the Silver City area and the Owyhees. An optional spur trail proceeds on a ridge for a clear northerly view. A number of conical rock towers punctuate the basin.

Complete the loop by descending off the ridge on the main trail and watch for a right-hand turn onto a faint two-track road three-tenths of a mile off the top. Turn right on the two-track and it crosses the mountainside above an aspen grove. At seven-tenths from the top, you'll come to a fence on a small saddle; turn left onto a two-track trail hugging the fenceline and follow it down Bonneville Gulch. It is a fast and fun downhill to the main road along Jordan Creek -- 1,000 feet of drop in less than two miles. At the bottom, the old Dewey Mine lies across the road. Turn left on the main road and ride eight-tenths back to the campground.

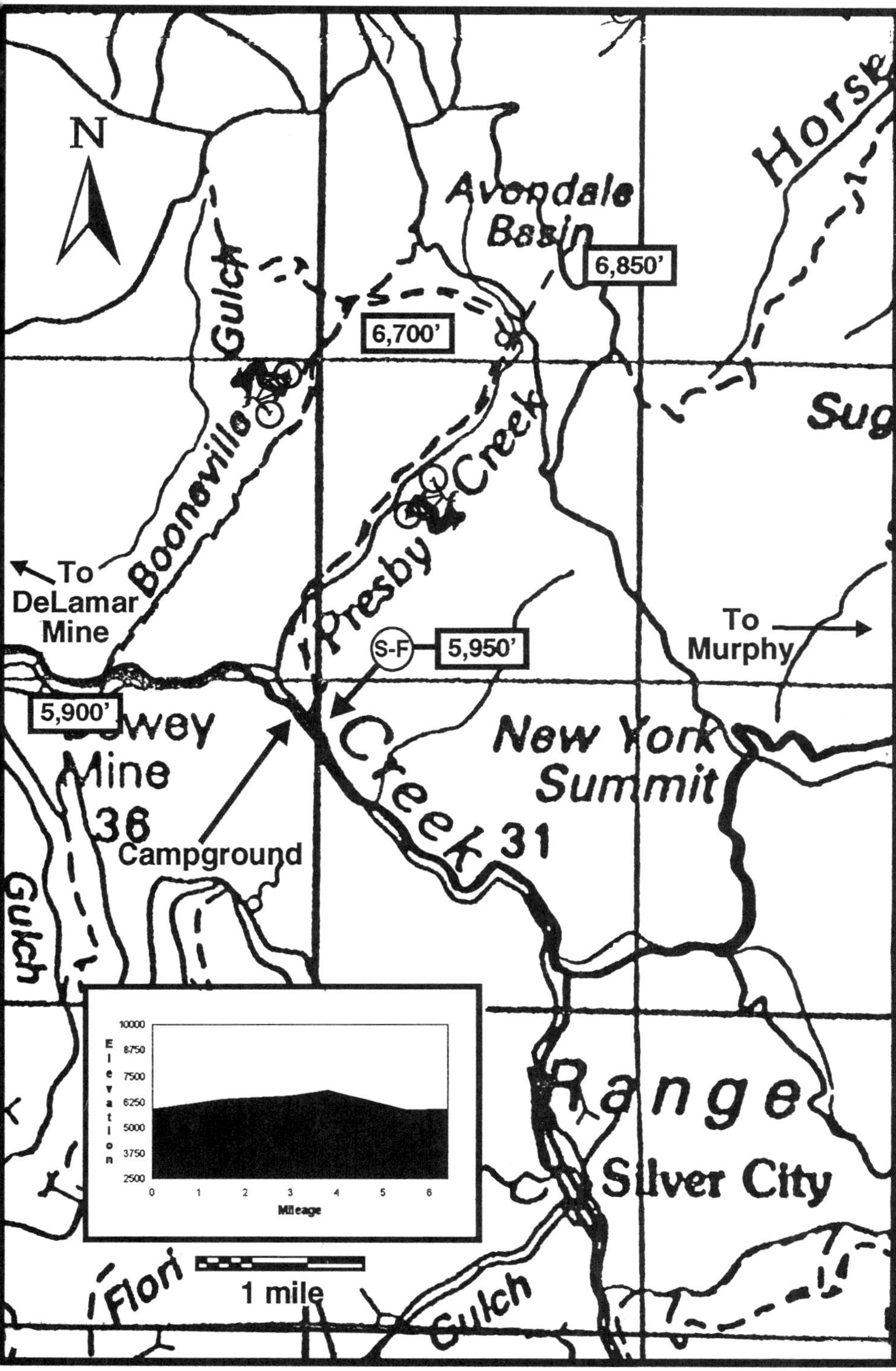
N
Horse
Avondale Basin
6,850'
6,700'
Gulch
Booneville
Presby Creek
Sug
To DeLamar Mine
To Murphy
S-F
5,950'
5,900'
Dewey Mine
36
Campground
Creek
31
New York Summit
Gulch
Range
Silver City
Flori
Gulch
1 mile
Elevation
Mileage
10000
8750
7500
6250
5000
3750
2500
0
1
2
3
4
5
6

EXPERT RIDES

CORRAL CREEK LOOP

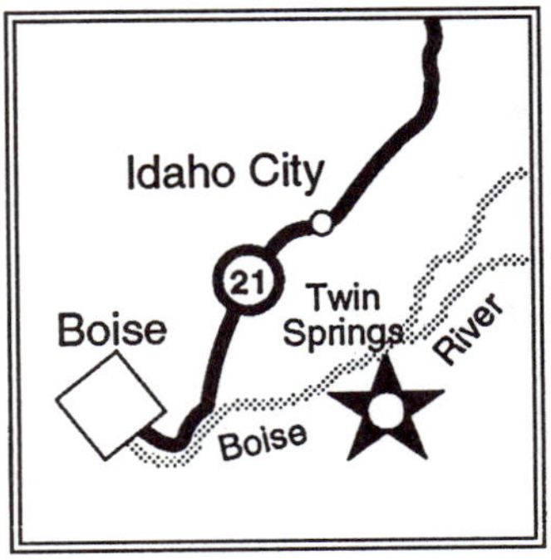

Quality: ***
Distance: 25.5 miles
Difficulty: Experts only
Riding time: 3.5-6 hours
Trail: 4WD road, single-track, 2WD road
Season: May-October
Watch out for: blazing heat/rattlesnakes
Topo maps: Long Gulch, Twin Springs

Getting there: From Boise, drive east on Idaho 21 about 15 miles, just past the Mores Creek bridge. Turn right on the Middle Fork Road (USFS Road #268) heading toward Atlanta. Drive 22.8 miles to the first bridge crossing the Middle Fork of the Boise River, turn right, cross the bridge and park.

The Ride: The Corral Creek loop is a thrilling challenge for expert riders who love to climb, but it's punishing route involving a 6.5-mile, unrelenting climb up Corral Creek on single track with little to no shade to protect you on a hot day. We recommend starting very early in the morning or riding this route on a cool day. The route starts with a 3.5-mile moderate ascent on the Long Gulch 2WD dirt road. Spin easy gears on this hill and conserve your energy for the Corral Creek grade. At a small summit, the 2WD road descends about 3.4 miles to the Corral Creek trailhead on the left. It is signed and called the Corral Creek-Reed Trail No. 129. Now you've got 10 miles of single track ahead. The trail involves a vertical gain of over 3,000 feet, including some grueling steeps of 600 feet or more per mile, to the top of a brushy ridge overlooking the Middle Fork country. Most riders will have to walk their bikes for the steepest sections of the climb. At just over 13 miles, the trail finally reaches the top, where you will enjoy splendid, 360-degree views, a good place for lunch. At about 14.4 miles, the trail forks: stay to the right. The descent into Sheep Creek is steep on a loose trail, but it's rideable. At 15.8 miles, turn right again to follow the trail into a big meadow. Sheep Creek trail is across the draw. At 16.05 miles, cross Sheep Creek on a wooden bridge; the Sheep Creek trail junction is 16.2 miles. Go left to head back to the Middle Fork road; it's a little over a mile -- mostly level or downhill -- to the Middle Fork road. When you reach the road, turn left and ride about 7.5 miles back to your rig. You may want to stop at Twin Springs for a cool drink.

Variations: Reverse the loop by starting at the Sheep Creek trailhead and riding up the Corral Creek trail from the Sheep Creek side. It's an even steeper climb -- most riders will have to walk their bikes on the loose trail -- involving a 3,300-foot rise over only three miles (ouch!). However, the upside is that you'll have a big downhill reward.

Interpretive remarks: Portions of Corral Creek and Sheep Creek burned in the summer of 1992; therefore, the shade factor on this ride is practically non-existent, and it's prime habitat for rattlesnakes. Watch for them when you're walking your bike.

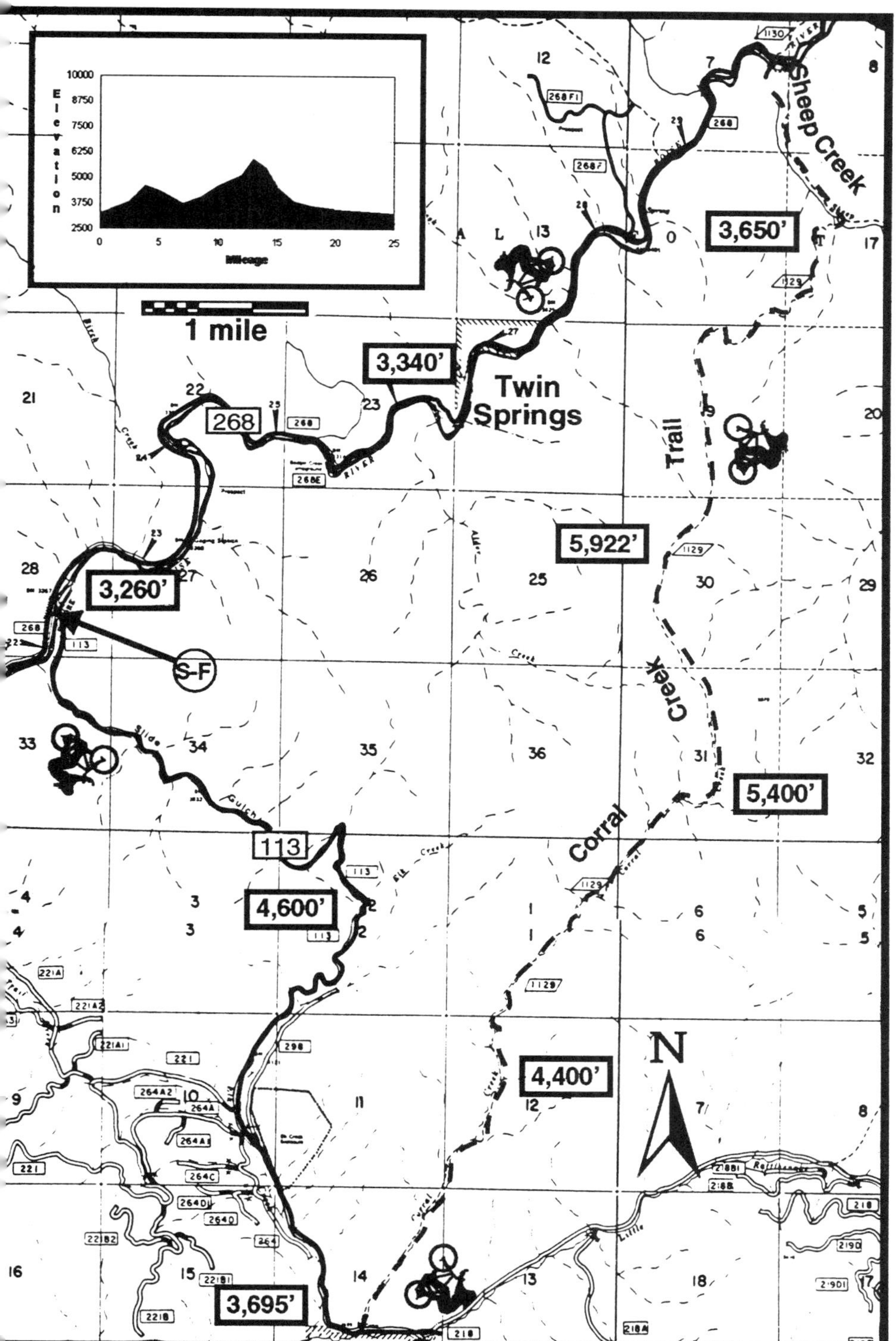

Elevation
Mileage
1 mile
Twin Springs
Sheep Creek
Trail
Corral Creek
3,650'
3,340'
3,260'
5,922'
5,400'
4,600'
4,400'
3,695'
S-F
268
113
N

COTTONWOOD CREEK LOOP

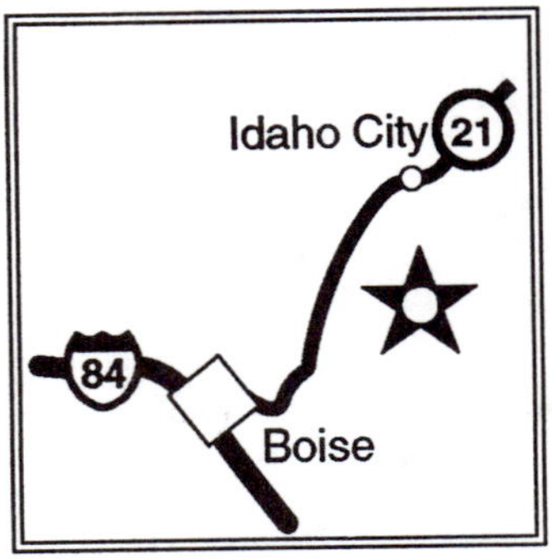

Quality: ****
Distance: 20.5 miles
Difficulty: advanced/expert
Riding time: 3-5 hours
Trail: Single-track, 4WD road, 2WD road
Season: May-October
Watch out for: heavy brush
Topo map: Arrowrock Reservoir

Getting there: From Boise, drive east on Idaho 21 about 30 miles to the Cottonwood Creek turnoff. Turn right and follow the dirt road about 7 miles to the Thorn Butte Lookout Road junction (USFS Road #203 and #377). Park your vehicle there. Ride 3.9 miles down USFS Road #377 to the Cottonwood Creek Trailhead on the left-hand side of the road. The trailhead is marked by a registration box and turnout. The ride starts here.

The Ride: Cottonwood Creek Trail is an excellent single-track ride along a beautiful, shaded creek bottom adorned with a wide variety of wildflowers, aspen and cottonwood trees, and a perennial stream. The trail climbs about 3,290 feet over 8.3 miles to the junction with the Thorn Creek Lookout road. Start the ride by picking up the trail behind the registration box and turn left along the hillside. The trail climbs at a reasonable grade most of the way -- about 400 feet per mile -- and features multiple creek crossings. Bridges cross the first three, but you've got to walk across the rest. The brush is heavy in places, at times forcing riders off the bike. Besides the creek crossings and brush, the trail is rideable for the first 6.5 miles or so. Then the grade increases to about 600-800 feet per mile. Only the most skilled and fit riders will be able to ride this section. At about 7.9 miles, the trail crosses the creek to the left and soon the gradient becomes more gentle, allowing riders to pedal the final half-mile to the road junction. A lush, green meadow near the summit rewards cyclists for the arduous climb. If you are so inclined, ride another .75 miles (450 feet of gain) on the jeep trail to Thorn Butte lookout for a heart-thumping, 360-degree view of the Boise National Forest. **Complete the loop** by taking Thorn Creek Lookout road eight miles down a brush- and tree-lined ridgeline to your vehicle. The jeep trail has multiple ruts and rocks. Keep your speed in check for hazards and hairpin corners. Stop occasionally on the way down to soak in the expansive view of the forest; watch for deer and elk grazing in the open meadows.

Variations: Reverse the loop by parking at the Thorn Creek Lookout Road-Cottonwood Creek Road junction, ride the jeep trail to the lookout or trail junction, and take Cottonwood Creek Trail down to the main road.

Interpretive remarks: A bounty of wildflowers decorates Cottonwood Creek for much of the climb. Among the flowers you will see in June include sagebrush buttercup (yellow), scarlet gilia (honeysuckle-like red, trumpet-shaped flowers) and blue penstamon (bluebell-shaped flowers).

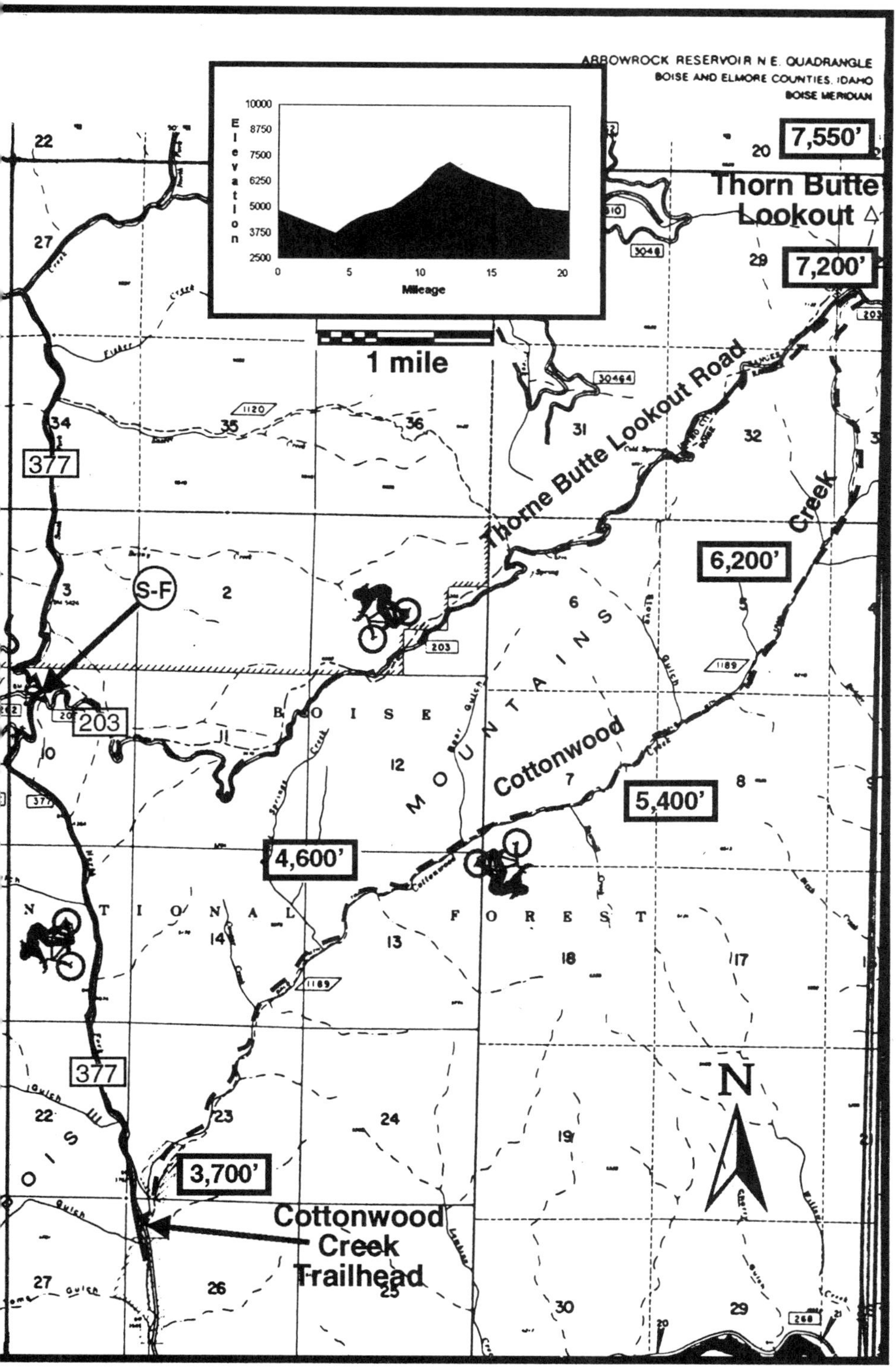
ARROWROCK RESERVOIR N.E. QUADRANGLE
BOISE AND ELMORE COUNTIES, IDAHO
BOISE MERIDIAN
Elevation
Mileage
10000
8750
7500
6250
5000
3750
2500
0
5
10
15
20
1 mile
7,550'
Thorn Butte Lookout
7,200'
Thorne Butte Lookout Road
Creek
6,200'
5,400'
Cottonwood
4,600'
3,700'
Cottonwood Creek Trailhead
S-F
377
203
BOISE
MOUNTAINS
NATIONAL
FOREST
N

TRAPPER CREEK LOOP

Quality: ****
Distance: 18.6 miles
Difficulty: Advanced
Riding time: 2.5-4 hours
Trail: 4WD road, single-track
Season: June-September
Topos: Grand Mountain, Bear River

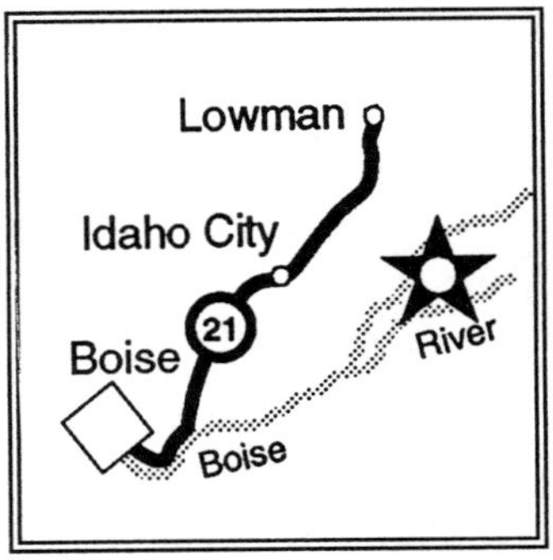

Getting there: From Boise, drive east on Idaho 21 about 65 miles to the Edna Creek Road (USFS Road #384), turn right. Follow the dirt road about 12 miles to the North Fork of the Boise River. Turn left and follow the road about three miles to the Trapper Creek logging road. The road is distinguished by a major concrete bridge crossing the north fork. Park so that you don't block the gate.

The Ride: The Trapper Creek logging road rises sharply right off the bat, but don't let it scare you off -- it climbs an average of less than 300 feet per mile over 9 miles to Grand Mountain, one of the most reasonable grades of any long uphill grade in this book. Less than a quarter mile up the road, the road rises at a 20 percent pitch and turns to pavement for a half mile. At .85 tenths, you reach a preliminary summit, the pavement ends, and the road drops for .6 tenths of a mile. At 1.4 miles, the road begins a long uphill ascent toward Grand Mountain at a very pleasant, consistent pitch. As the road climbs and wraps around the mountain, the views of the surrounding countryside get better and better. At 7.7 miles, the road reaches the saddle, watch for a trail blaze in the trees on the left -- that's the beginning of the single-track trail. The trail is rideable for all or most of the way for advanced or expert riders. At mile 9.26, you skirt Granite Mountain and begin an invigorating descent along a gentle, broad pine-covered ridge. Watch for blazes in the trees to stay with the trail in places where it gets sketchy. At mile 12.39, you reach the trailhead and a green wooden post that says, "Trail." It's another mile to the Trail Creek dirt road. Turn left and cruise back to Trapper Creek on the North Fork road; be sure to turn left at Deer Park after crossing the North Fork of the Boise River at mile 14.6.

Interpretive remarks: Riders may wonder why the first part of the road is paved. Forest Service officials say they experimented with the pavement to reduce erosion during a logging operation.

Other activities: Camping, hiking, fishing, whitewater boating (in the spring), tubing in the summer, photography.

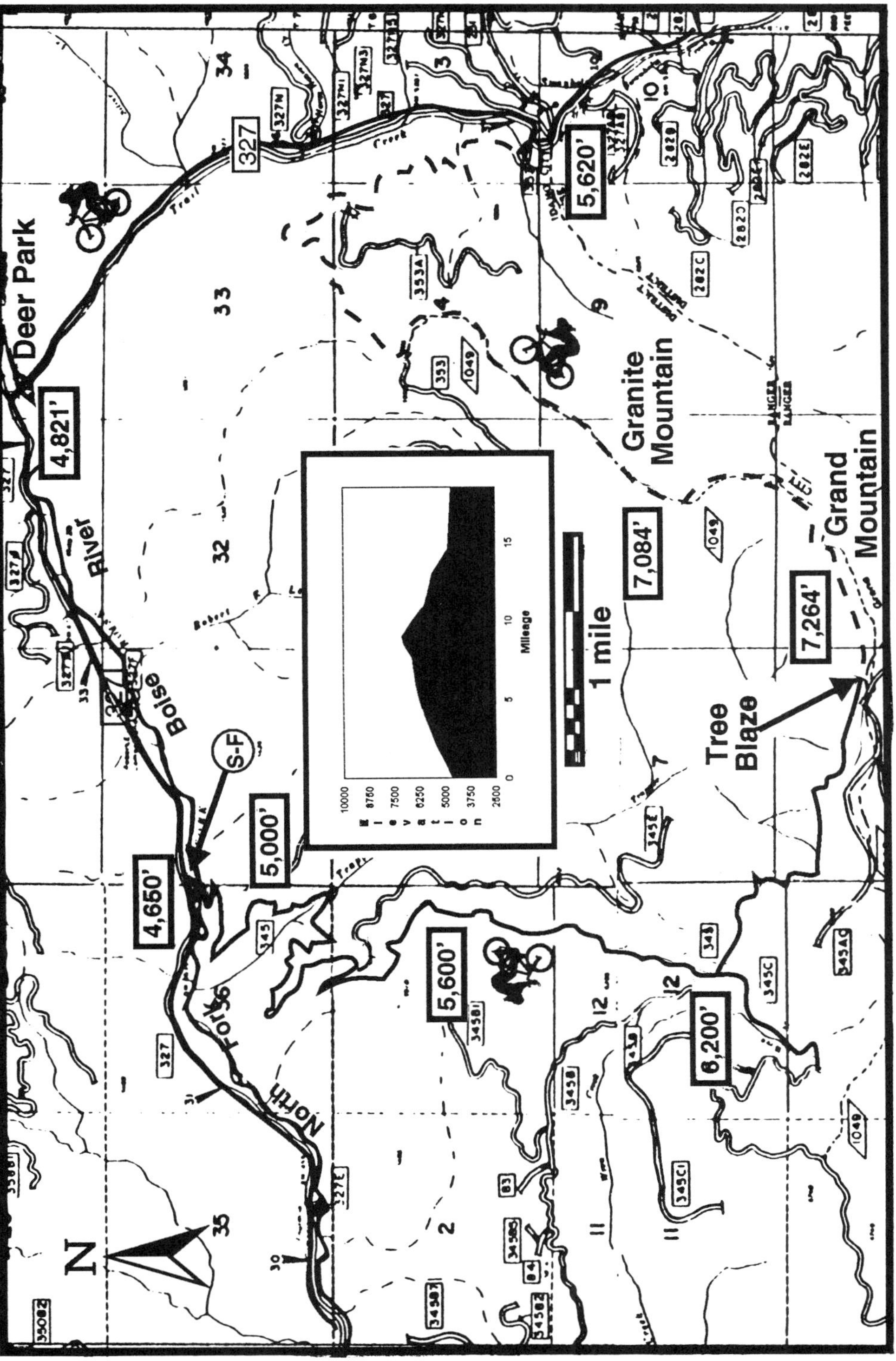

Deer Park
4,821'
327
Boise River
North Fork
S-F
4,650'
5,000'
5,600'
5,620'
Granite Mountain
7,084'
7,264'
Grand Mountain
6,200'
Tree Blaze
1 mile
Mileage
N

GRIMES 311 LOOP

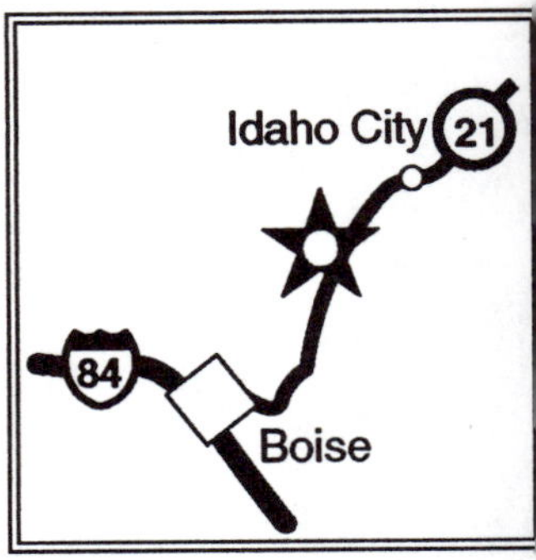

Quality: ***
Distance: 31 miles
Difficulty: Advanced
Riding time: 3.5-4.5 hours
Trail: Single-track, 4WD road
Season: May to mid-October
Watch out for: Huge ruts and water bars in the road.
Topo maps: Idaho City, Warm Springs

Getting there: From Boise, drive east on Idaho 21 about 30 miles to the Grimes Creek turnoff and historical sign. Turn left and park. The ride starts here.

The Ride: The 311 loop provides a wealth of diversity for cyclists -- it starts with a warm up on pavement, rolls through an historic mining town and finishes with an exhilarating downhill on a high ridge. Start the ride by pedaling 10.25 miles on Idaho 21 to Idaho City. Turn left and ride up main street and watch for the left-hand turn to Centerville. Climb about 3 miles on the 2WD dirt road to a marked left-hand turn for Forest Service Road #311. Turn left and follow the road. For the next 6.5 miles, the road heads uphill most of the way, but the climbs are interspersed with a few downhill sections that allow for rest and recovery. As the road narrows, the descent becomes long and steep, with numerous water bars and ruts to keep your interest. Road #311 is the only well-established road down the ridge. Be sure to stay on the main road and ignore spurs peeling off to the left or right. After 23 miles, the road levels out and weaves along the hillside. Then a final descent drops to the Grimes Creek Road and your vehicle.

Variations: Cyclists can avoid riding on the busy, dangerous highway by dropping a vehicle on Grimes Creek Road, and driving to Idaho City or the #311 junction. Then, the ride distance is reduced to about 20 miles.

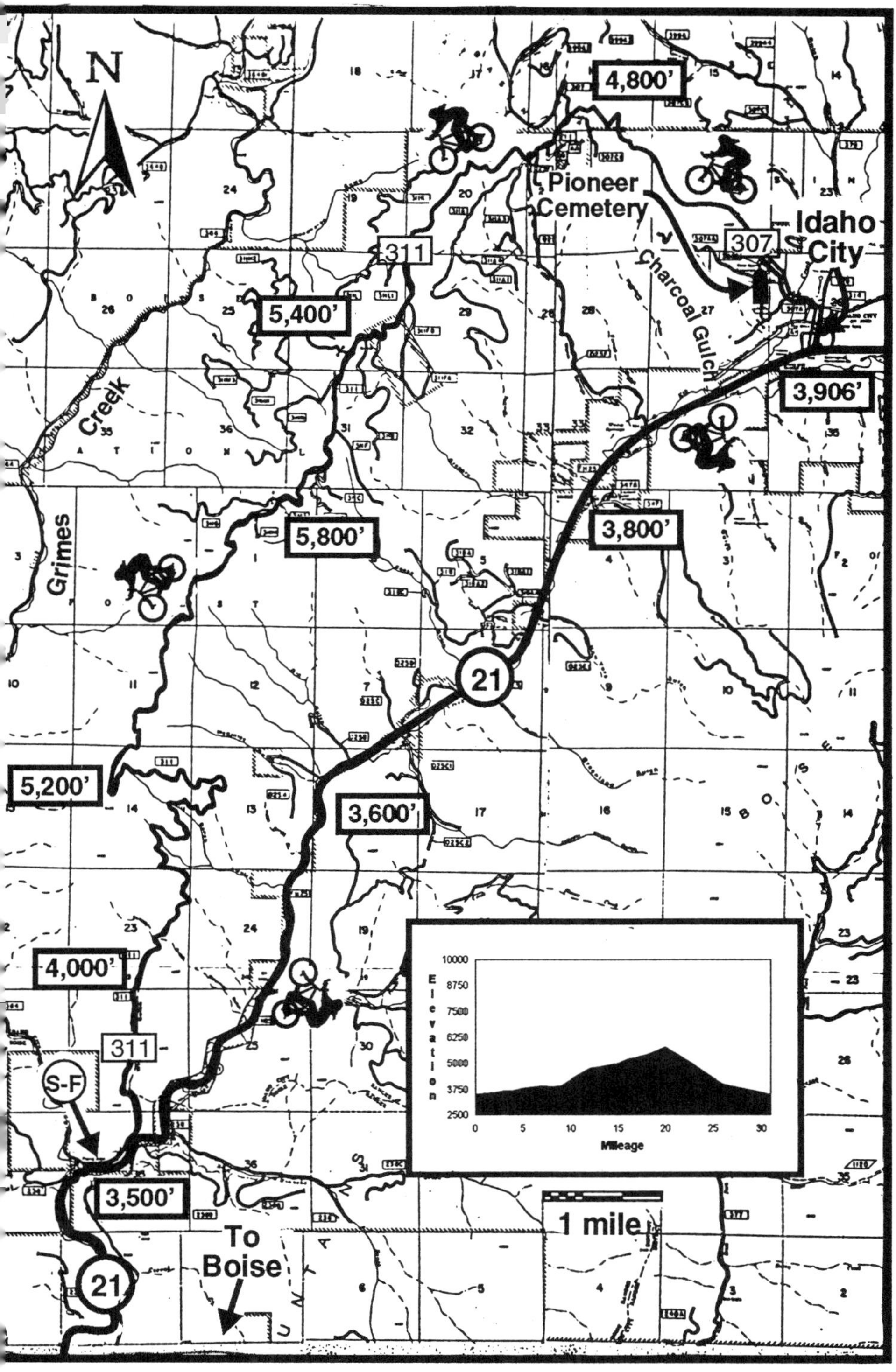
N
4,800'
Pioneer
Cemetery
Idaho
City
307
311
Charcoal Gulch
5,400'
3,906'
Creek
Grimes
5,800'
3,800'
21
5,200'
3,600'
4,000'
311
S-F
3,500'
To
Boise
21
1 mile
Elevation
10000
8750
7500
6250
5000
3750
2500
0
5
10
15
20
25
30
Mileage

WEST MOUNTAIN-JOE'S CREEK LOOP

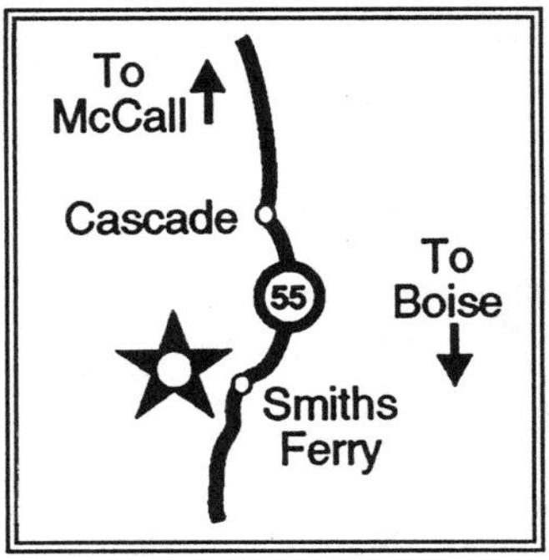

Quality: ***
Distance: 21.5 miles
Difficulty: Advanced/Expert
Riding time: 3-5 hours
Trail: Single-track, 4WD road, 2WD road
Season: June-October
Topo map: Smith's Ferry

Getting there: Drive about 55 miles north of Boise on Idaho 55 to Smith's Ferry. Across from the Cougar Mountain Lodge, there is a well-marked road leading to Sagehen Reservoir and High Valley. Turn left and head for Sagehen. About five miles up the road, you will climb to a forested summit and see a sign on the right-hand side of the road for the West Mountain Trail. Park. The ride starts here.

The Ride: This is an arduous loop ride that involves a 2,200-foot climb to Tripod Lookout over 6.6 miles. From the start, the trail drops into the forest immediately, crosses a creek, and then climbs steeply toward a series of undulating meadows on a broad ridge. In some of the steeper pitches, some riders will have to walk. At times, the trail is very sandy, making climbing difficult and tiresome. At 2.3 miles, riders break out of the forest and the lookout comes into view. From here, the trail descends into another clump of trees and winds along the ridge -- this is one of nicest parts of the uphill ride. At about 4.7 miles, the trail crosses a big draw and climbs steeply for the lookout. For most of the next mile, the trail is too steep, brushy, rocky or sandy to ride. Over this distance, it climbs about 800 feet--too steep for even the most gonzo riders. But it's worth the walk because you're almost to the top. At 5.7 miles, the trail intersects Joe's Trail; it's about a eight-tenths to the lookout. The view on top is stupendous, a 100-mile panorama of southwest Idaho. Look for the Sawtooths to the east, Granite Mountain and the Seven Devils to the north, Long Valley (McCall to Cascade), the West Mountain spine, and Hitt Mountain, Council Mountain, Cuddy Mountain and the Wallowa Mountains in Oregon to the west. It's a very big view. **Now the descent begins** as you plunge to the Joe's Creek intersection and follow Joe's, a single-track path, toward Sagehen. Take it slow in the steep areas because the trail splinters and rolls over rocks and tree roots. About 2.5 miles down Joe's Trail, the single-track ends and you'll fly about 3.5 miles down a logging two-track road to the reservoir. Near the lake, Joe's Creek trail intersects a paved road, turn left, and head for one of three campgrounds (Sagehen Creek, Eastside, Hollywood Point) for access to the lake for a swim. If you didn't shuttle a car, someone will have to ride 8 miles (1,200 feet of vertical gain) back to the car.

Variations: Once you're on top, you can cruise on the West Mountain trail toward Wilson Meadows and Snowbank Mountain. From there, you could scream down the Cabarton Road, a 2WD dirt road (USFS Road No. 446), to the Clear Creek store on Idaho 55. If you've got an extra driver handy, they could meet you there.

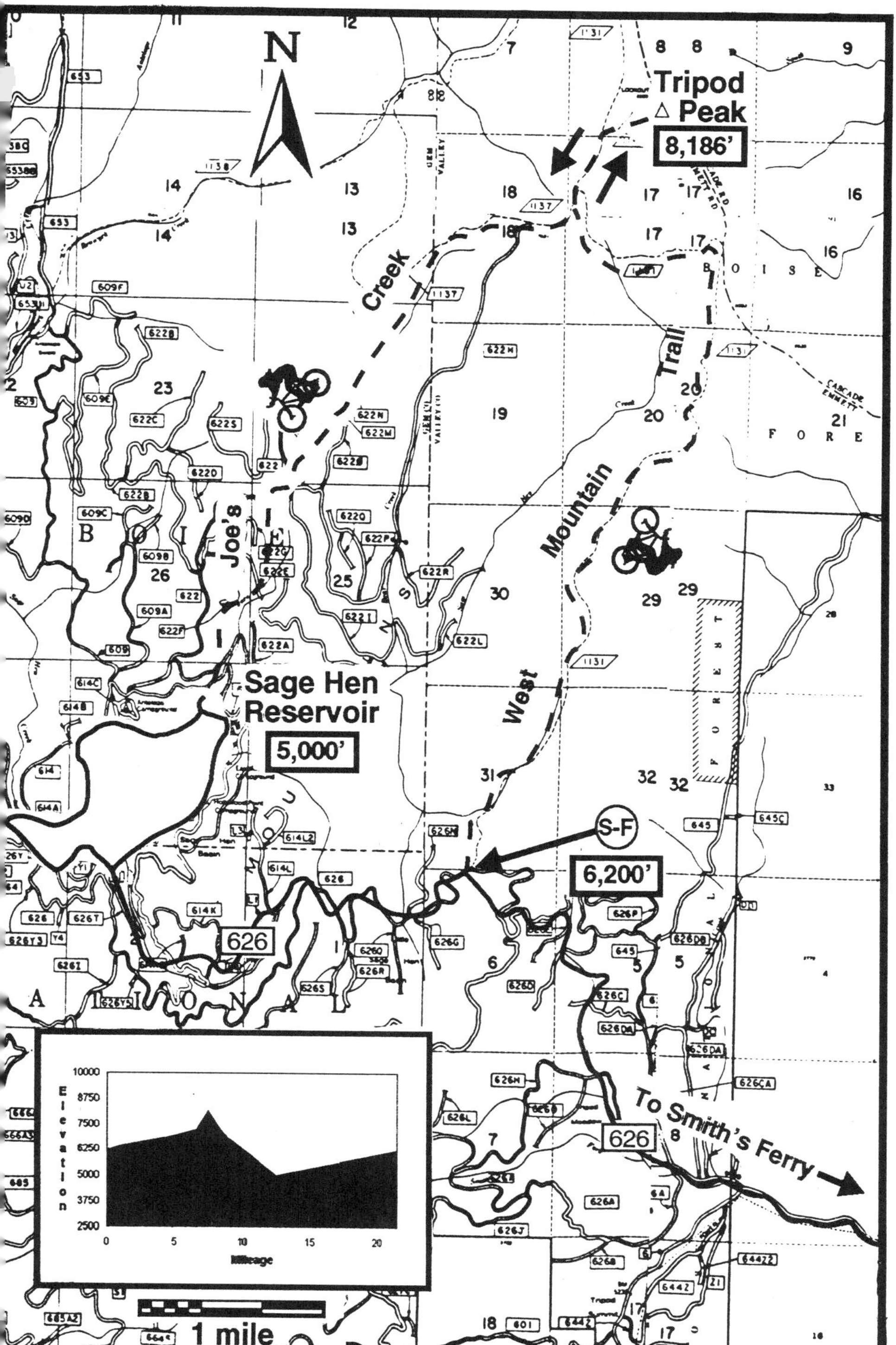

N
Tripod Peak
8,186'
Creek
Trail
Mountain
West
Joe's
Sage Hen Reservoir
5,000'
S-F
6,200'
626
To Smith's Ferry
Elevation
Mileage
1 mile

HIGHLAND VALLEY LOOP

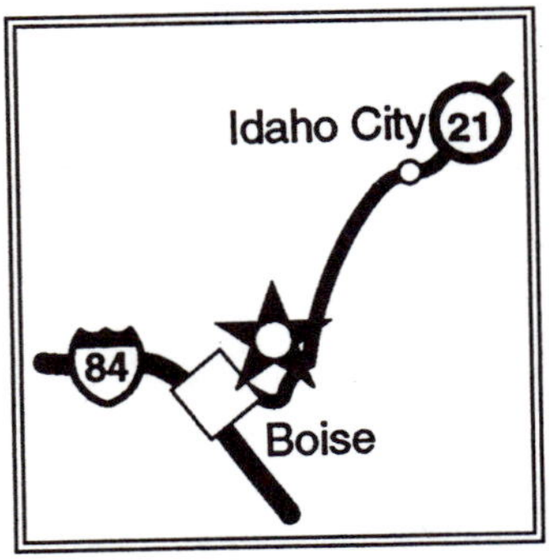

Quality: ***
Distance: 25.5 miles
Difficulty: Advanced
Riding time: 3-5 hours
Trail: Paved path, dirt 4WD road
Season: May-October
Topo: Lucky Peak, Robie Creek

Getting there: Ride the Greenbelt to Discovery Park and Lucky Peak (it's 8.5 miles from Municipal Park). At the end of the path, turn right on Idaho 21 and climb 3 miles to Highland Valley Road on the left-hand side. Turn left on Highland Valley. Those who want to shorten the ride could drive to this point and park in the large pulloff on Idaho 21.

The Ride: Highland Valley Road rises at a fairly steep pitch -- over 2,000 vertical feet -- in 5.5 miles to the top of Lucky Peak (elevation 5,900 feet). But once over the top, cyclists can look forward to a long downhill for about nine miles back to Boise via Rocky Canyon Road. Start up Highland Valley Road from Idaho 21. The 4WD road starts out at an enjoyable pace for the first couple miles. At 1.3 miles, Highland Valley Road turns left and Trail E begins on the right. Take Trail E and begin the climb to Lucky Peak. At mile 2.3, a junction with Trail 8 and E appears, go right and follow Trail E. A STEEP hill rises from the junction for 3/10ths, then the grade slackens a little. At mile 3.1, the Trail 9 junction peels off to the right. Stay left and climb some more. At mile 3.8, Trail 9 appears again, stay left on Trail E and make the final ascent to Lucky Peak. You've got 700 vertical feet to climb in about 1.4 miles. At mile 5.2, cyclists cross a cattle guard near the top. Soak in the easterly view of the Sawtooths and Boise River headwaters. At mile 5.4 is a T-junction, turn right and you're over the top now, heading down toward Aldape Summit. The trail descends along the terraced mountain slope and follows the ridge spine. At mile 5.8, Trail 8 reappears, go straight and remain on Trail E. At mile 6.3, cyclists reach the summit of the forested knob, it's downhill all the way now. At mile 7.24 is a four-way junction, bear left and stay on Trail E. It's two miles of downhill to Rocky Canyon Road. At mile 9.3, cyclists reach the junction with Rocky Canyon, turn left (unless you want to climb to Aldape, it's less than a mile) and cruise down the road back to Boise. It's 5.5 miles back to Shaw Mountain Road.
Interpretive remarks: Extensive man-made terraces can be seen as riders descend from Lucky Peak to Rocky Canyon Road. The terraces were constructed in the early 1960s following a major wildfire on Lucky Peak and ensuing heavy rains and flooding in east Boise. Grass and trees were planted in the terraces to keep the soil in place. Today, officials say, such draconian measures would not be taken.

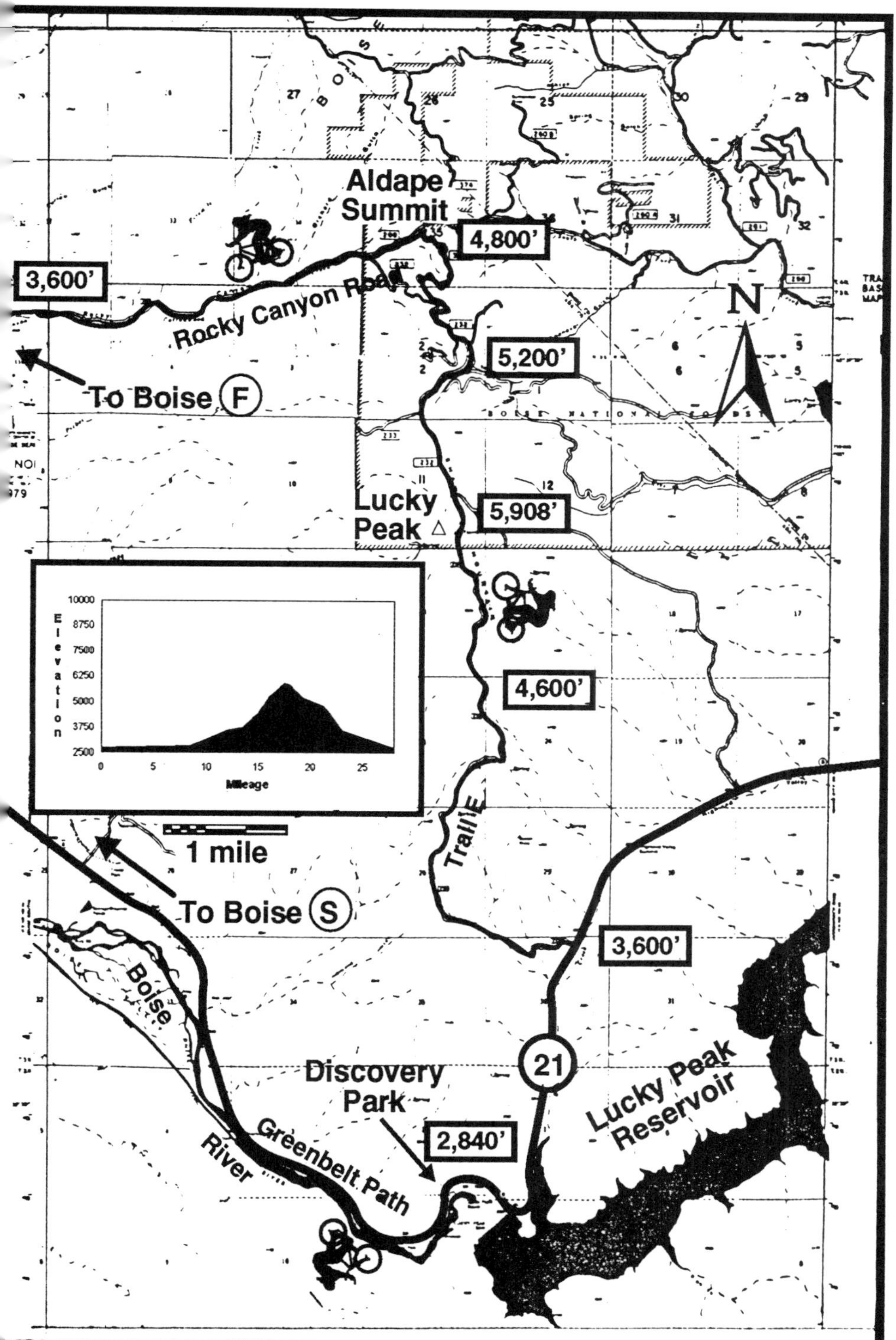
Aldape Summit
4,800'
3,600'
Rocky Canyon Road
5,200'
To Boise F
N
Lucky Peak
5,908'
4,600'
Elevation
Mileage
1 mile
Trail E
To Boise S
3,600'
Boise
21
Discovery Park
Lucky Peak Reservoir
2,840'
Greenbelt Path
River

EAGLE NEST TRAIL

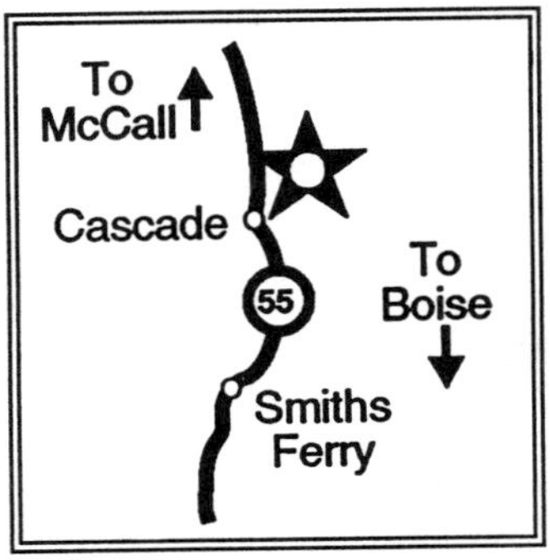

Quality: ****
Distance: 18.2 miles
Difficulty: Expert
Riding time: 3.5-5.5 hours
Trail: Single-track; 4WD road
Season: Late May-October
Caution: Trail is technical; stay alert.
Topo map: Eagle Nest

Getting there: From Boise, drive north on Idaho 55 about 70 miles to Cascade. Proceed through town. Watch for a right-hand turn for Warm Lake about one mile north of town. Turn right and head for Warm Lake 6 miles to the junction of USFS Road #400 and Highway 22. Turn left onto #400 and park. The ride begins here.

The Ride: Eagle Nest Trail is a challenging, enjoyable route that wanders like a giant serpent through dense old-growth forest. It features a vertical gain of 2,000 feet over about 7.2 miles, and several steep in-your-face climbs. From the car, ride up #400 about 3.8 miles (estimated). Watch for a small sign on the right-hand side of the road indicating Eagle Nest trail #111. Turn right on the single-track trail. You'll climb a steep grade for several hundred yards. Follow the trail for about 3.5 miles to the summit. At 7.3 miles (approximate), watch for a dirt road on the left. Drop off the trail to the road (the trail never joins it), and turn left (south). You are now back on the #400 road. Follow the road to the 14.3 mile point and note the junction where you left the road in the first place. Continue down the #400 road about 3.8 miles to your vehicle. Return as you came.

Interpretive remarks: The authors had originally logged this ride going up the Eagle Nest trail from the Crawford work station. But the Boise National Forest decided to close this small area to public use to provide exclusive privacy for a few Forest Service employees. By closing the area, the Forest Service blocked public access to the Eagle Nest Trail. We objected, but to no avail. Therefore, we provided an alternative route on the #400 road; the mileage is approximate as the closure occurred in mid-November after snowfall had buried the trail. Beyond the Crawford site, the Eagle Nest trail is on state Endowment Land, meaning the revenues from logging the area go toward funding the state's universities and public schools. New logging projects may occur in the area and possibly disrupt the trail, but the authors have expressed an interest with state authorities to preserve the trail for public recreation.
Combo activities: Camping, fishing, hiking, boating. Take a side trip to Warm Lake, Cascade Reservoir or Horsethief Reservoir.

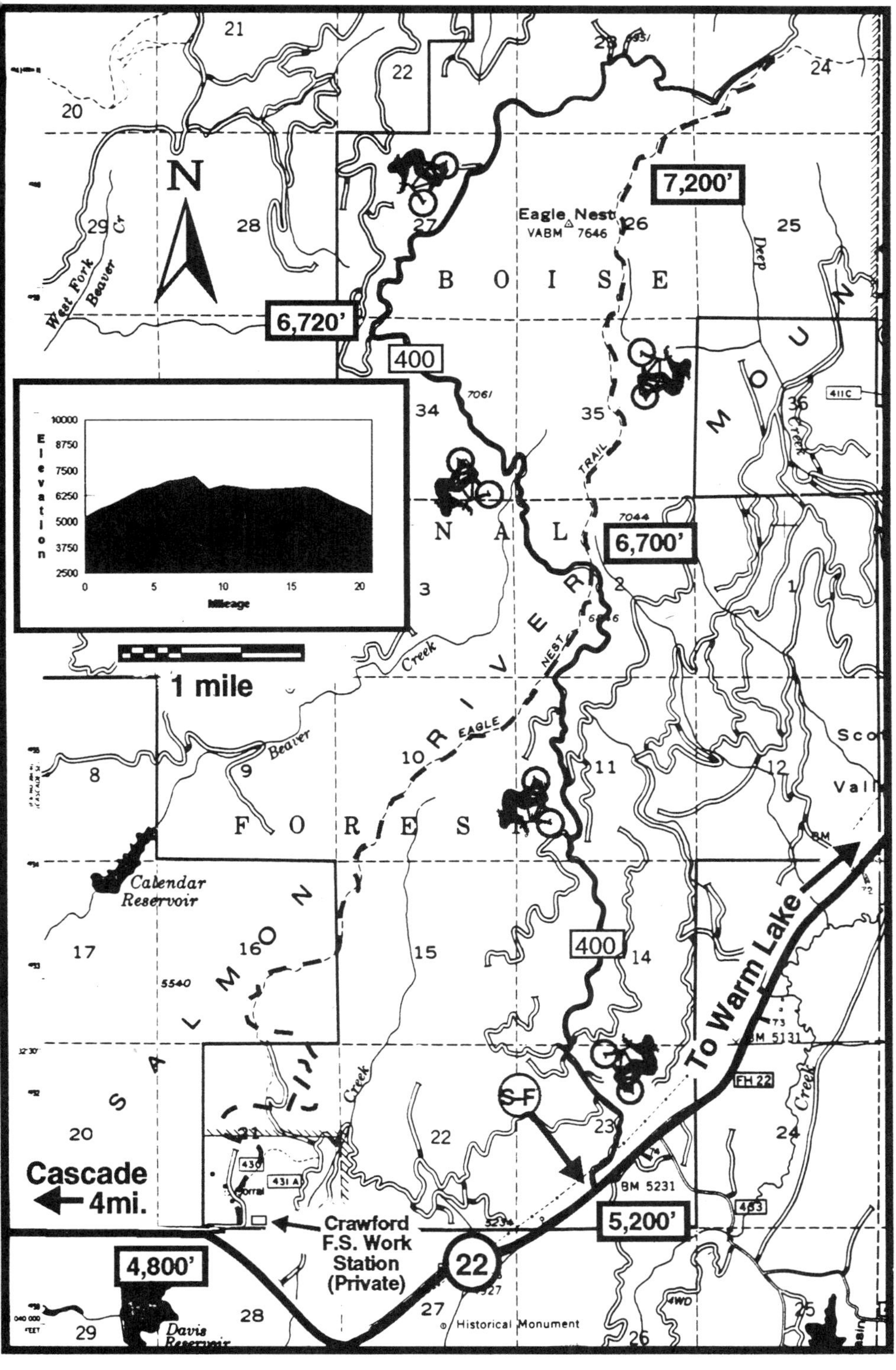

N
7,200'
Eagle Nest
VABM 7646
6,720'
400
BOISE
NATIONAL
RIVER
FOREST
SALMON
MOUN
6,700'
EAGLE NEST TRAIL
Elevation
Mileage
1 mile
Beaver Creek
Calendar Reservoir
To Warm Lake
FH 22
S-F
Cascade 4mi.
Crawford F.S. Work Station (Private)
5,200'
4,800'
22
BM 5231
Historical Monument
Davis Reservoir

RUBY MEADOWS-LOON-SECESH LOOP

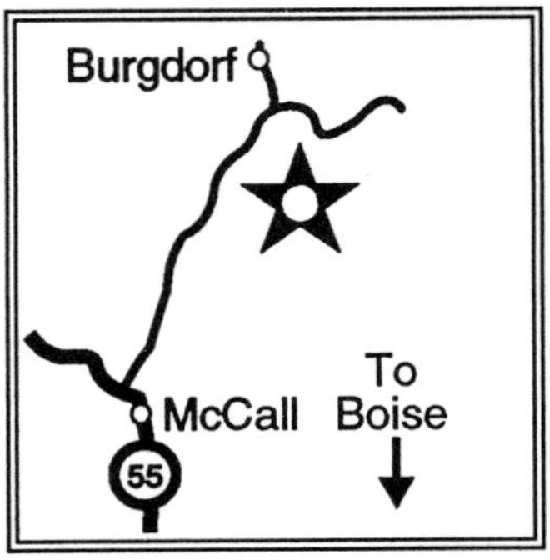

Quality: ****
Distance: 21 miles
Difficulty: intermediate/advanced
Riding time: 3-6 hours
Trail: Single-track, 4WD road
Season: June-October
Topo maps: Burgdorf SE and SW, Victor Peak, Loon Lake.

Getting there: Go north on Idaho 55 to McCall; proceed through town to Warren Wagon Road (just after Shore Lodge), turn right. Follow the road about 28 miles, past Secesh Summit, to a sign for Ruby Meadows on the right side of the road (the turnoff to Burgdorf is across the road. Turn right and follow the 2WD dirt road to a pullout (within the first quarter-mile) and park. The ride starts here.

The Ride: This is a beautiful loop ride on mostly single-track trail through thick alpine forest and spongy meadows to Loon Lake and the Secesh River. Bring a lunch; it's a long ride that deserves a nice easy pace to enjoy in the scenery. The ride begins with a short section of rocky 2WD dirt road and then climbs abruptly for seven-tenths of a mile. Then it's a quick downhill to the beginning of Ruby Meadows and a creek crossing. In low water, it's possible to ride across the stream. From there, the two-track jeep trail meanders through a lodgepole pine forest next to the meadows. Ignore roads branching off on the right, unless you want to take a side trip. At 4.6 miles, the road intersects the Loon Lake/Willow Basket Creek trail, go left. It's 6 miles to the lake. The single-track trail descends along Willow Basket Creek and provides views of small meadows and a subalpine fir, lodgepole pine forest. At 8.3 miles, the Loon Creek trail intersects the Victor Creek trail, and Trail No. 081 leading to Chinook Campground. Go straight, cross the bridge, and head for Loon Lake, it's 1.5 miles ahead. The trail climbs steeply to the lake, but it's rideable. Just before the lake, riders will enter a meadow less than one-quarter mile away. It's an easy jaunt to the lakeshore from there for a magnificent view. Listen for the chilling, giggling call of the loon. On the way back, take the right fork in the meadow to the Secesh River. It's a quick two miles to the river, involving some excellent single-track descents. Cross the bridge and go left. It's four miles to Chinook Campground on this well-maintained single-track trail. It climbs and falls along the Secesh River. In July and August, look for summer chinook salmon holding in the pools; the threatened fish rest there on the 750-mile journey home from the Pacific Ocean. The trail is rideable the whole way. At Chinook Campground, the route returns to a 2WD dirt road for nine miles back to the rig. Follow the road exiting the campground to the Warren-Secesh highway, turn left. It's a slightly uphill cruise to Ruby Meadows.

Possible variations: Drive to Chinook Campground (go straight past Ruby Meadows and Burgdorf) and do a short loop between the campground and Loon Lake. Take Trail No. 081 on the way to the lake, and Trail No. 080 on the way back. This loop requires crossing the Secesh River (don't try it in high water).

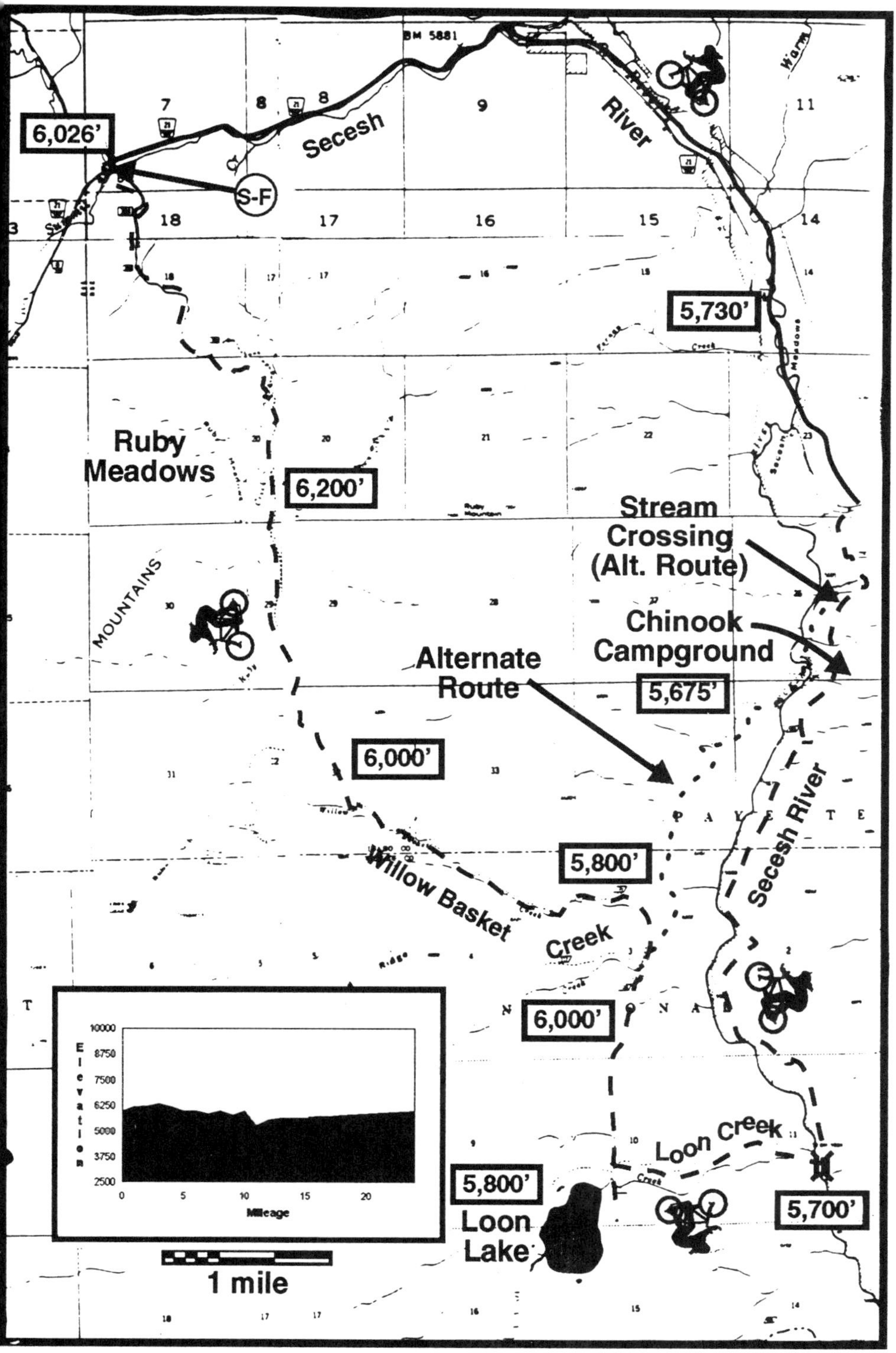
6,026'
Secesh
River
S-F
Ruby
Meadows
6,200'
MOUNTAINS
5,730'
Stream
Crossing
(Alt. Route)
Chinook
Campground
Alternate
Route
5,675'
6,000'
5,800'
Willow Basket
Creek
Secesh River
6,000'
Loon Creek
5,800'
Loon
Lake
5,700'
Elevation
Mileage
1 mile

IDAHO CITY BANZAI LOOP

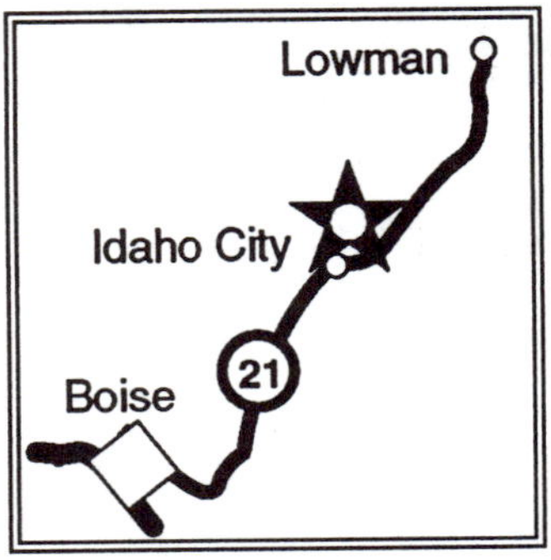

Quality: ****
Distance: 20 miles
Difficulty: Expert
Riding time: 2-4 hours
Trail: 2WD road, 4WD road, single-track
Season: April-October
Topo maps: None available.

Getting there: Drive to Idaho City on Idaho 21 from Boise. Turn left at the visitor's center and drive up main street to the brick school. The ride starts here.

The Ride: This ride offers a wonderful variety of trails, terrain and scenery in the Idaho City area, but it involves 36 turns and even more junctions. Riders who attempt this ride MUST have a cyclocomputer; the authors recommend that cyclists ride this loop with someone who has ridden it before. From the school, cross main street and ride up Bear Run Road, past Duquette Pines, for several miles. At mile 3.4, turn right. At mile 3.8, go left on 4WD road and climb steep pitch. At mile 4.1, turn right onto 2WD road. At mile 4.2, turn right at a large ponderosa pine onto single-track trail and follow it for three-tenths. At mile 4.5, turn right on 2WD road (back on Bear Run). At mile 4.8, turn right on 4WD road. At mile 5.2, turn right onto jeep trail. At mile 5.5, turn left onto single-track trail (be sure to duck underneath large pine tree hanging over the trail). At mile 6.1, turn left onto jeep trail. At mile 6.4, turn left onto single track for a short climb. At mile 7.1, turn right onto jeep trail next to an old mine. Follow it for a half mile, and turn left onto single track. Proceed on the trail for over a mile. At 8.7 miles, cross jeep trail and stay on single-track. At mile 9, turn right onto 4WD road. At mile 9.7, turn right onto single track for steep climb. At mile 10.4, turn left onto jeep trail. At mile 10.5, go straight. At. mile 11.4, proceed across dirt road and stay on jeep trail. At mile 11.5, turn left onto single track for almost a mile. At mile 12.3, turn left and plunge to a crossing of Idaho 21. Cross the highway and ride up Granite Creek road. At mile 13, turn right off the main road onto a jeep trail. At mile 14.2, turn right onto single track. At mile 14.4, stay right on single track. At mile 14.9, go left. At mile 15 is a three-way junction, go right across the creek. At mile 15.3, turn left up main 2WD road for a mile. At mile 16.4, turn right across small creek marked by big culvert and rusty gate. You're entering state land on a jeep trail. At mile 16.8, turn right. At mile 17.5, turn left. At mile 18.2, turn right onto single track trail. The turn is marked by scattered logs, a skinny pine tree on the left with orange paint on it. The narrow trail drops steeply through old mining areas and thick timber. At mile 19.4, turn left off logging road onto single track. At mile 19.7, turn left at single track junction (be careful in short steep drops). At mile 20.1, the trail crosses Mores Creek. Proceed to the right through Jackson's log deck to Tom's Service Station and Idaho City main street. Return to the school. This trail was custom pioneered by Dale Sweet, a Idaho City mountain biker, for the Banzai race series. Thanks Dale!

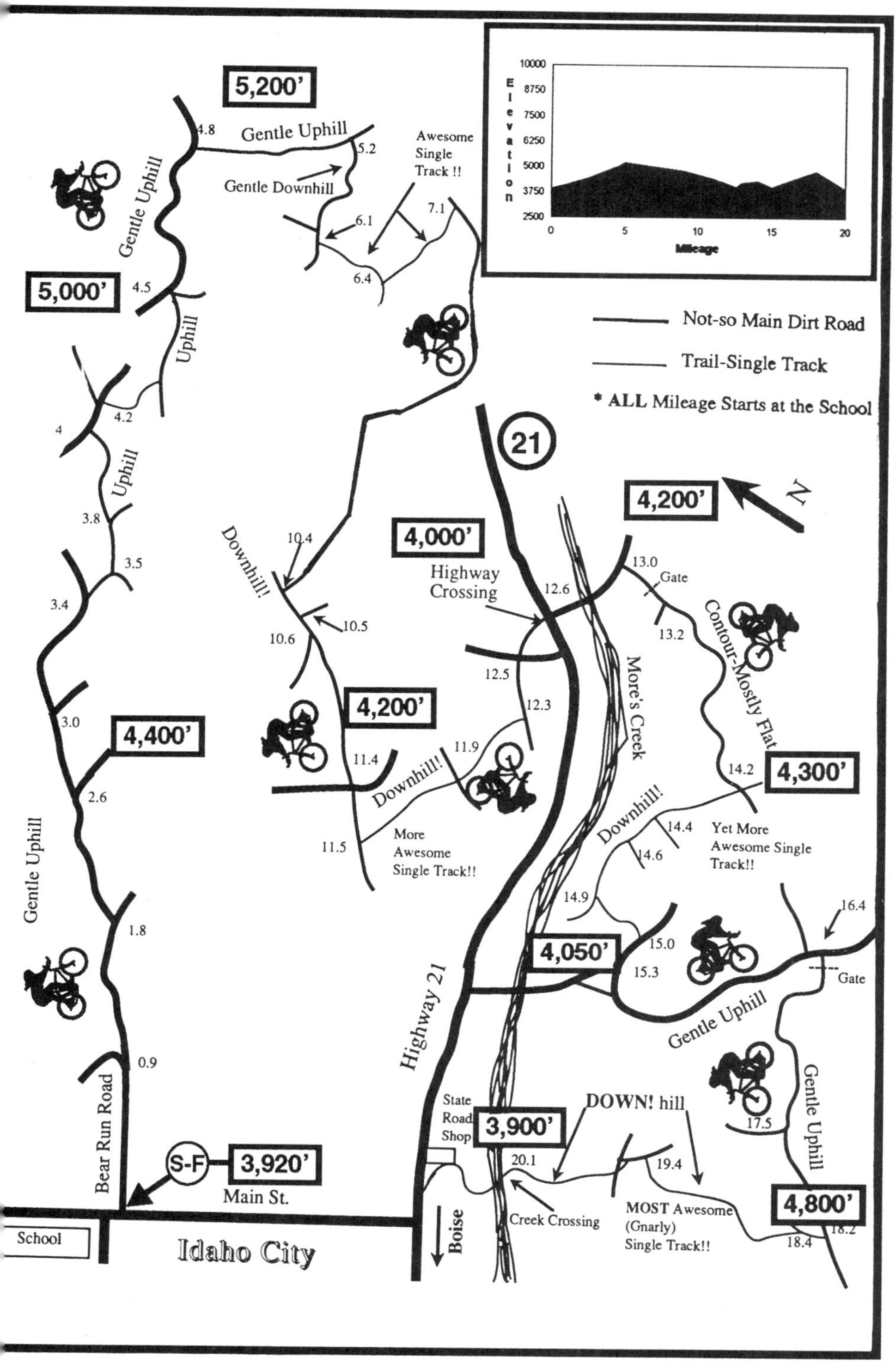

5,200'
5,000'
4,400'
4,200'
4,000'
4,300'
4,050'
3,900'
3,920'
4,800'
Gentle Uphill
Gentle Downhill
Uphill
Awesome Single Track !!
Downhill!
Highway Crossing
More Awesome Single Track!!
Contour-Mostly Flat
Yet More Awesome Single Track!!
More's Creek
Highway 21
21
Gate
DOWN! hill
MOST Awesome (Gnarly) Single Track!!
Creek Crossing
State Road Shop
Bear Run Road
S-F
Main St.
School
Idaho City
Boise
Not-so Main Dirt Road
Trail-Single Track
* ALL Mileage Starts at the School
N
Elevation
Mileage
10000
8750
7500
6250
5000
3750
2500
0
5
10
15
20
0.9
1.8
2.6
3.0
3.4
3.5
3.8
4
4.2
4.5
4.8
5.2
6.1
6.4
7.1
10.4
10.5
10.6
11.4
11.5
11.9
12.3
12.5
12.6
13.0
13.2
14.2
14.4
14.6
14.9
15.0
15.3
16.4
17.5
18.2
18.4
19.4
20.1

DEADWOOD-JULIE CREEK LOOP

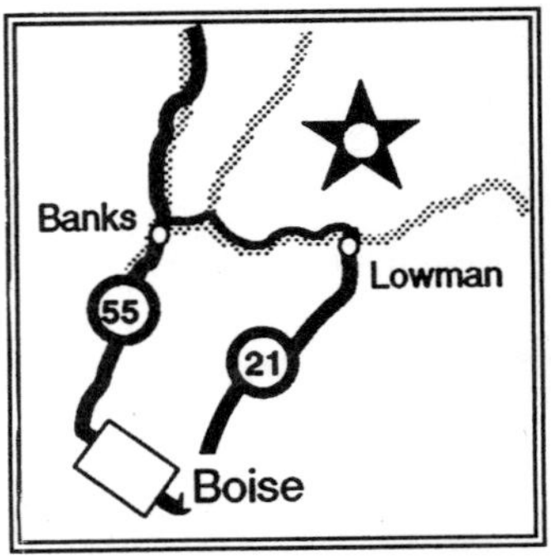

Quality: ****
Distance: 24.5 miles
Difficulty: Expert
Riding time: 3.5-6 hours
Trail: Single-track, 2WD road, hike-a-bike
Season: May-October
Watch out for: Steep climbing!
Topo maps: Pine Flats, Eight-Mile, Scott Creek

Getting there: From Boise, drive north on Idaho 55 for 34 miles to Banks. Cross the bridge over the South Fork Payette River and turn right. Proceed on the Banks-Lowman Road for about 30 miles to the Deadwood Campground on the left-hand side of the road. The campground is about seven miles west of Lowman. Park. The ride starts here.

The Ride: The Deadwood Loop involves a steep, arduous 12-mile, 3,200-vertical-foot climb up the Deadwood Ridge, but the hard work is rewarded by an exhilarating descent down Julie Creek and a scenic ride along the Deadwood River back to the start. If you like to climb, this ride is for you. The trailhead begins from the small campground and rises straight up the steep ridge spine for the first half-mile. Most riders will have to walk part of the steep stuff and don't sweat it -- you've got a long climb ahead. After the first mile, the grade eases a little so that it's rideable for experts, and the trail winds through a shaded ponderosa pine and Douglas-fir forest offering nice vistas of the opposite ridge. But it's still a tough first-gear grind for the first seven miles. At mile 7, the trail reaches a saddle of sorts and drops for 2.5 miles on the west slope of the ridge for a rewarding change of pace. At mile 9.5, the trail crosses a creek over a primitive wooden bridge and then climbs some more toward a junction at mile 11.3 with the trail to Stevens Point. It's less than a mile to the signed Julie Creek junction on the high ridgetop. This is a good place for lunch and a long rest. It's nearly all downhill from here back to the campground. The single-track trail drops 2,500 vertical feet in five miles or so to the Deadwood River. Go slow on the switchback corners, watch for rocks and other trail users, and keep your speed in check to avoid trail damage. From Julie Creek trailhead, a 2WD road winds for seven miles along the Deadwood River back to the campground.

Combo activities: The Deadwood Campground is also the jumping off point for the "canyon" section of the South Fork Payette River, an expert-only run for rafts and kayaks. Bring your camping and boating gear and spend a day on the river after your grueling ride. Also, fishing, hiking, and hot springs at Pine Flats Campground.

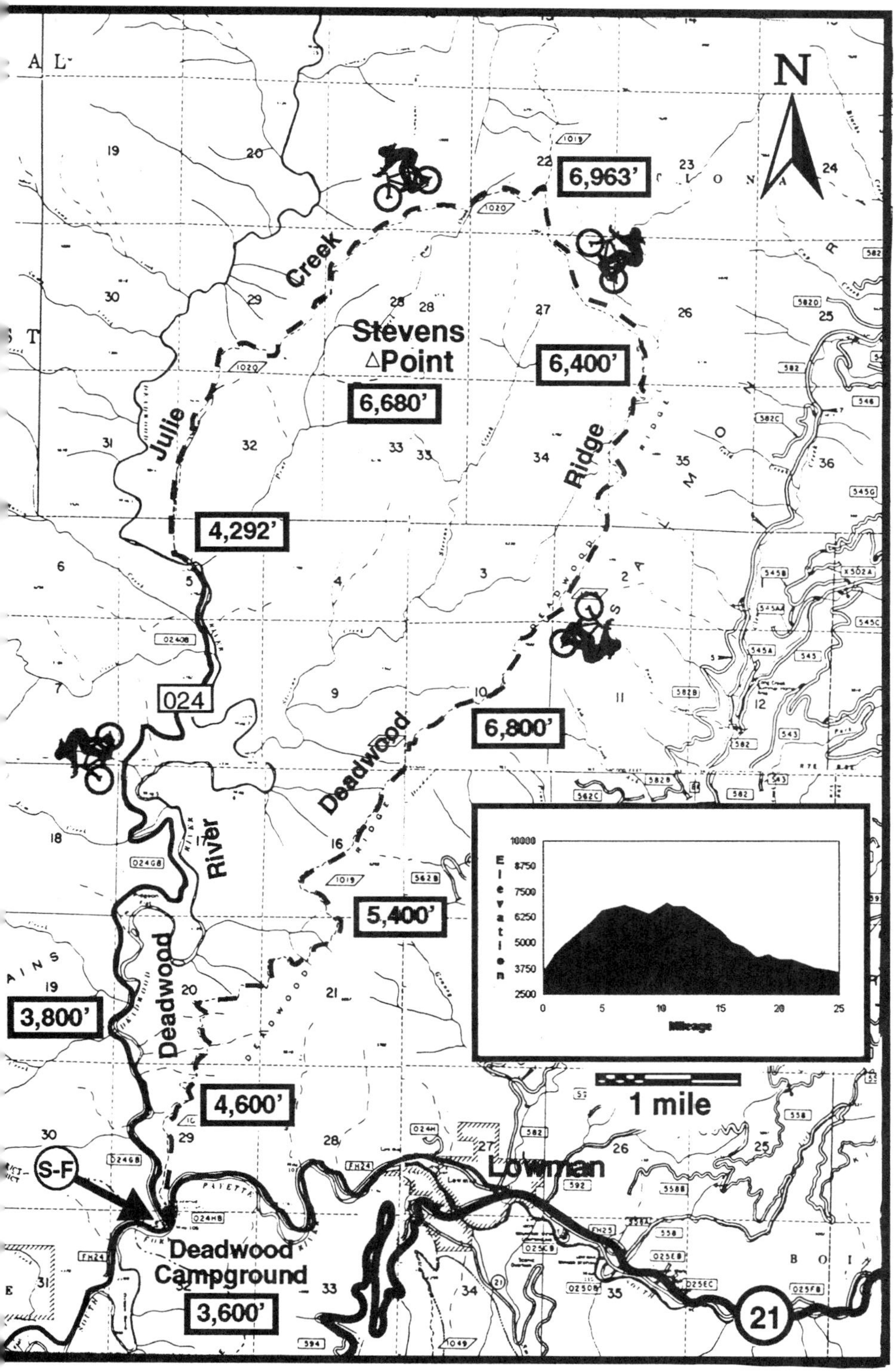
N
6,963'
Creek
Stevens
Point
6,680'
6,400'
Julie
Ridge
4,292'
024
Deadwood
6,800'
River
5,400'
Deadwood
3,800'
4,600'
1 mile
S-F
Lowman
Deadwood
Campground
3,600'
21
Elevation
10000
8750
7500
6250
5000
3750
2500
0
5
10
15
20
25
Mileage

WARM SPRINGS PLUNGE

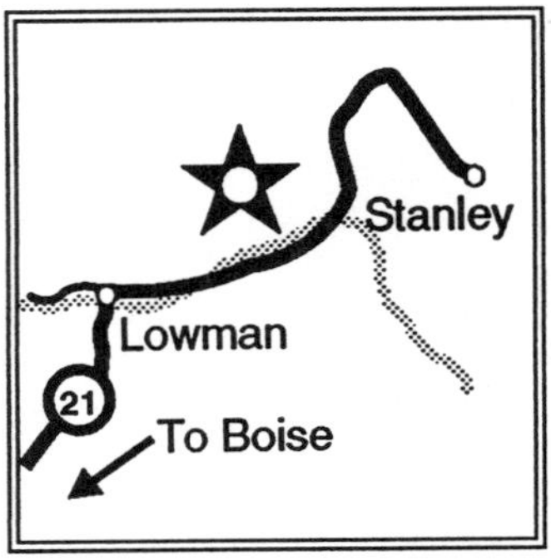

Quality: ****
Distance: 15 miles
Difficulty: Advanced
Riding time: 2.5-4 hours
Trail: All single-track
Season: June-October
Caution: Steep descents on narrow trail
Topo maps: Bull Trout Point, Eight-Mile

Getting there: From Boise, drive northeast toward Stanley on Idaho 21 about 95 miles (just past Banner Summit) to a well-marked left-hand turn to Bull Trout Lake. Park in a pullout near the highway. The ride starts here. Note: This ride requires a hitchhike or shuttle back to the Bull Trout Lake. If you have a large group, drop a vehicle at Bonneville Campground, the end of the ride.

The Ride: The Warm Springs trail involves an invigorating, 2,325-vertical-foot descent from Bull Trout Lake (elevation 6,950) to Bonneville Campground (elevation 4,625). However, the ride involves some challenging steep climbing along Warm Springs Creek. In short, it's not all downhill. To begin the ride, cruise toward Bull Trout Lake (about 1.7 miles) to the Warm Springs Trailhead. It's well-marked on the right-hand side of the road. From here, it's single-track riding all the way. The trail winds past Bull Trout Lake (stay right and ignore spur trails peeling off to the left) and climbs for the first 1.5 miles to a small summit overlooking Dead Man Creek. Here begins a steep, 1,200-vertical-foot plunge for the next three miles down the narrow basin. The trail drops along steep mountainsides -- be careful of sandy, loose soil. About 4 miles into the ride, the trail reaches Warm Springs Creek, a broad alluvial plain, and bends left. From here, the trail rolls up and down along the creek for the next 8 miles. Near mile 7, the trail crosses Warm Springs Creek on a wooden bridge. Near mile 9, the trail crosses a side creek that has blown out into a big gully. You'll have to walk across it. At mile 12.5, the trail begins to climb at a steep pitch out of the canyon for the next mile or so. Some riders may have to walk. Near mile 14.5, you'll reach a junction with Link Creek trail, stay left to drop down to Idaho 21 by the entrance of the campground. A half-mile later, go left again to skirt the guard station and drop into the campground area.

Combo activities: Hit the hot springs at the head of the campground for a soothing soak after the hard ride. Camping, fishing, whitewater boating, hiking.

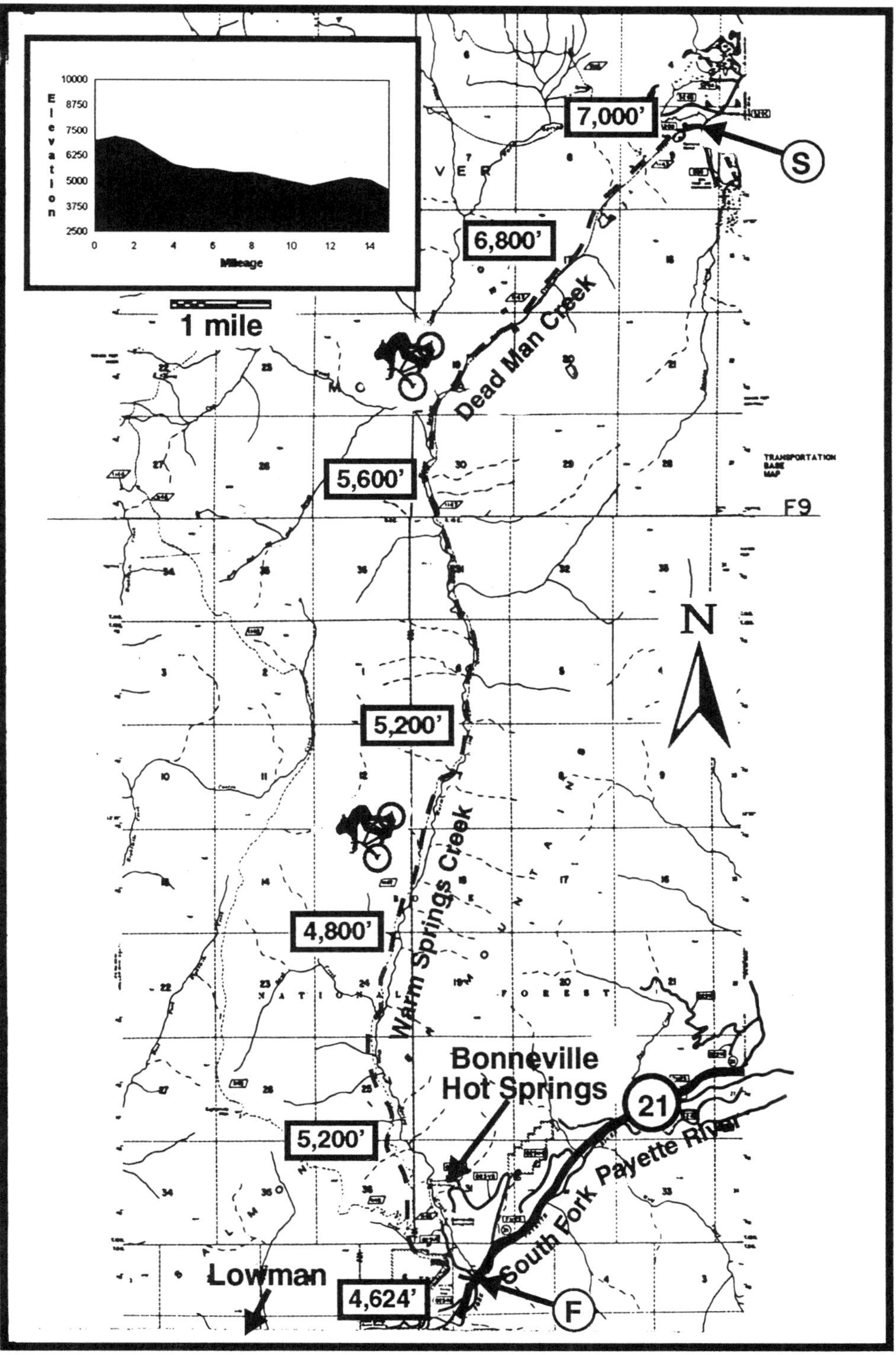

10000
8750
7500
6250
5000
3750
2500
Elevation
0 2 4 6 8 10 12 14
Mileage
1 mile
7,000'
S
6,800'
Dead Man Creek
5,600'
TRANSPORTATION BASE MAP
F9
N
5,200'
Warm Springs Creek
4,800'
Bonneville Hot Springs
21
5,200'
South Fork Payette River
Lowman
4,624'
F

COULTER SUMMIT LOOP

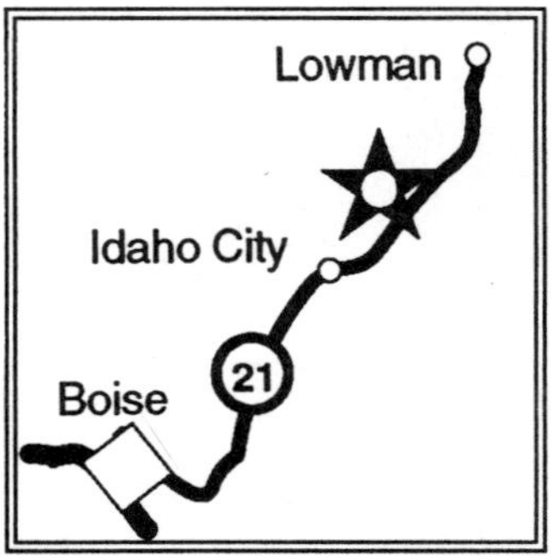

Quality: ****
Distance: 19.8 miles
Difficulty: Expert
Riding time: 3.5-4.5 hours
Trail: Single-track, 4WD road
Season: Mid-May to mid-October
Topo maps: Sunset Mountain, Pioneerville

Getting there: From Boise, drive about 50 miles east on Idaho 21, past Idaho City, to Mores Creek Summit. Park in the large lot on the right-hand side of the highway.

The Ride: The Coulter Summit loop provides a scenic tour of the upper Grimes Creek watershed and features a nearly equal amount of climbs and descents. Ride across the highway and head for Pilot Peak on Forest Service Road #380. It's 3.2 miles to a saddle junction. Stay on the main road that bends to the right (do not take the immediate right-hand turn to Pilot Peak). At 3.4 miles is the junction of Bear Run Road; turn left and ride a half-mile to another fork. Take the right fork, which passes an old mining cabin at 4.05 miles. At 4.4 miles, turn right, leave the main road and descend on a short technical downhill grade. Then the road rises sharply up a ridge. Follow the ridge and pass through several small meadows. At just over 5 miles, watch for a right-hand turn marked by a rock cairn. Please take a moment to improve the cairn and pile a few rocks on top. Turn right, hugging a rocky sidehill to the left of the cairn (the trail is sketchy here) and join a faint jeep trail. Follow the trail down two short steep drops and then begin climbing at 5.75 miles to a summit at 6.5 miles. Follow the trail into a large meadow and watch for sharp right-hand turn at 6.8 miles marked by a pile of rotten timbers. From here, cyclists cruise mostly downhill. At mile 8.9, a fork appears in the trail, stay right. At mile 9.1 is the junction of Wilson Peak and Coulter Summit trails, turn right on #380 and follow it back toward Pilot Peak. At mile 14, ignore the Rock Creek fork and stay on #380. At 16.3 miles, cyclists return to the junction of Bear Run Road and #380. Turn left and descend back to the parking lot.

Variations: Several sidetrips are possible on this ride. At the 6.8-mile junction (pile of rotten timbers), cyclists can proceed on the main trail to Wilson Peak. It's 1.7 miles one-way. Another option is to ride to the top of Pilot Peak Lookout. It's 8/10ths of a mile one-way from the saddle junction.

Combo activities: Wildflowers abound in the alpine meadows during July and August; wildlife watching; camping.

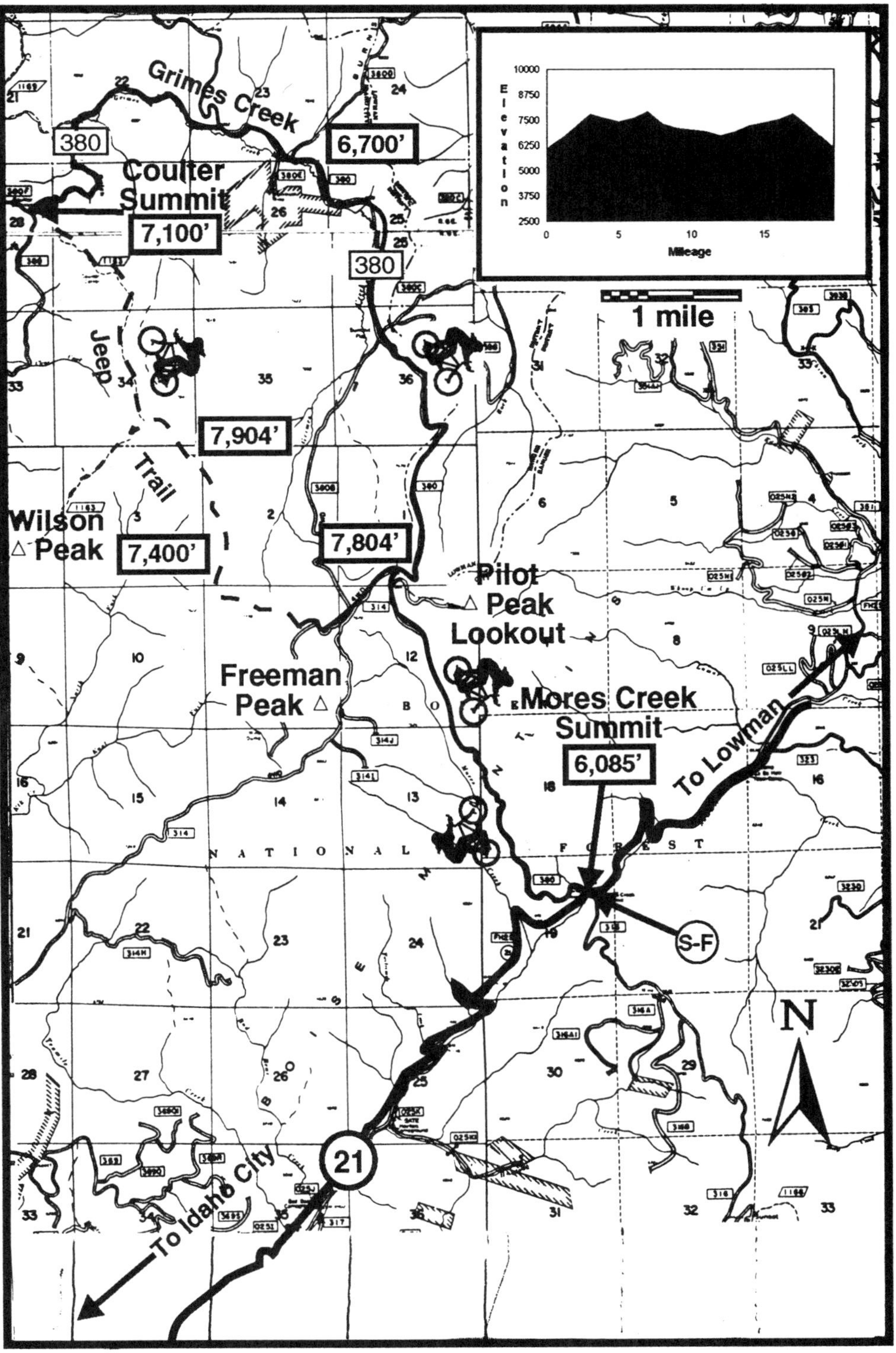
Grimes Creek
380
6,700'
Coulter Summit
7,100'
380
Elevation
10000
8750
7500
6250
5000
3750
2500
0
5
10
15
Mileage
1 mile
Jeep Trail
7,904'
Wilson Peak
7,400'
7,804'
Pilot Peak Lookout
Freeman Peak
Mores Creek Summit
6,085'
To Lowman
S-F
N
21
To Idaho City

INFORMATION/KEY CONTACTS

GREENBELT--Concerning the Greenbelt in the city of Boise, contact the Boise Parks System, 384-4240. In Garden City, call 377-1831. In Ada County, call 343-1328.

BOISE NATIONAL FOREST--Supervisor's office in Boise, 364-4100; Boise Ranger District, 364-4241; Idaho City Ranger District, 364-4330; Cascade Ranger District, 364-4270; Mountain Home Ranger District, 364-4310; Emmett Ranger District, 364-7000; Lowman Ranger District, 364-4250.

PAYETTE NATIONAL FOREST--Supervisor's office in McCall, 634-0700; McCall Ranger District, 634-0400; New Meadows Ranger District, 347-2141; Council Ranger District, 253-4215; Weiser Ranger District, 549-2420.

BUREAU OF LAND MANAGEMENT-BOISE DISTRICT--For information on trails in the Owyhees and Boise Front, call 384-3300.

BUREAU OF LAND MANAGEMENT-VALE DISTRICT--For information on desert trails in eastern Oregon, 503-473-3144.

RIDGE-TO-RIVERS TRAIL COORDINATOR--For information on trails in the Boise Front and Boise area, contact Tim Breuer, 384-3360.

IDAHO PARKS AND RECREATION DEPARTMENT--For information on state parks, 327-7444.

MOUNTAIN BIKE CLUBS

WOMBATS -- Women's Mountain Bike and Tea Society, Jacquie Phelan, founder, P.O. Box 757, Fairfax, Calif., 94978; Sarah Phipps, Boise chapter coordinator, 362-9644.

INTERNATIONAL MOUNTAIN BICYCLING ASSOCIATION--Address: Route 2, Box 303, Bishop, Calif., 93514.

LOCAL CLUBS--A number of mountain bikers are working on developing an advocacy organization in southwest Idaho to promote education, help maintain trails and work on access issues, among other things. For more information, contact Tim Breuer (see above) or Leo Hennessey at state parks (see number above).